WHITE AMONG THE REDS

The Author in 1946.

White Among the Reds

MASHA WILLIAMS

With twenty-seven photographs

SHEPHEARD-WALWYN

© Masha Williams 1980

All rights reserved

First published in 1980 by
Shepheard-Walwyn (Publishers) Limited
51 Vineyard Hill Road, London SW19 7JL

British Library Cataloguing in Publication Data

Williams, Masha, *Lady*
   White among the reds.
   1. Allied Commission for Austria
   I. Title
   943.6'05'0924   DB99.1
ISBN 0–85683–044–5

Typeset by
Input Typesetting Limited
Printed in Great Britain by
Whitstable Litho Limited, Kent

Contents

	List of Illustrations	vii
1	Arrival in Vienna	1
2	A Foreign and Rather Terrifying Atmosphere	8
3	Russian Obstruction?	18
4	Everything Suspended	30
5	Meeting of the Commanders-in-Chief	43
6	We Were Dismayed	46
7	The ACA gets down to Work	52
8	High-Level Entertainment	63
9	Cold Living	79
10	Marathon Conferences	87
11	Life Returning to Normal	97
12	The Commandants	106
13	Trips with Alec	121
14	Talking to the Russians	131
15	White Russians	137
16	High-Level Interpreting	147
17	The Iron Curtain	155
18	Spring Feeling	162
19	Change of Commanders-in-Chief	172
20	Something British and Good	177
21	My Engagement	186
22	Our Wedding	197
23	Last Days in Vienna	205
	Senior members of the Allied Commission for Austria referred to in the book	215
	Index	216

To
Libet and Lawrence

List of Illustrations

	The Author in 1946	Frontispiece
I	General Rogov and orphan adopted at Stalingrad	11
II	The Author wearing her Union Jack brooch	11
III	The British Headquarters, Schönbrunn Palace, in 1945	35
IV	Graves of Russian and Austrian soldiers killed in the battle for Vienna*	35
	Unveiling of the Red Army War Memorial 1945	
V	The Mayor of Vienna speaking	38
VI	Allied Generals	38
VII–IX	Red Army troops marching past	38–39
X	British troops, unarmed, marching past	39
XI	Meeting of the Russian and British C-in-Cs, Marshal Koniev and Gen. McCreery with Gen. Packard (centre) and interpreter (right)	47
XII	Schönbrunn Palace floodlit for a reception	71
XIII	The Author in conversation with the Russian C-in-C, Marshal Koniev*	74
XIV	Reception at Schönbrunn Palace. Gipsy violinist in the foreground*	75
XV	Brig. Verney, Brig. Palmer and Col. Gordon-Smith	107
XVI	Russian and French Commandants, Generals Lebedenko and Du Peyrat	111

XVII	Anniversary of the Liberation of Vienna Parade 1946 C-in-Cs inspecting troops†	166
XVIII	Russian Band in uniforms designed by Gen. Winterton†	166
XIX	Soviet troops marching past the C-in-Cs†	167
XX	French Chasseurs Alpins marching past C-in-Cs†	167
XXI	Troops marching from Red Army War Memorial†	170
XXII	Gen. Lebedenko, Marshal Koniev, Gen. Mark Clark, Gen. Winterton, Chancellor Figl and Herr Gruber before the Memorial†	170
XXIII	Gen. Kurasov arriving for the Tattoo dinner at the Schönbrunn Palace†	183
XXIV	The Author interpreting for British C-in-C, Gen. Steele, to Russian C-in-C, Gen. Kurasov, and his ADC Capt. Beloussov†	183
XXV	The Author's wedding in the Russian Orthodox Church in Vienna	203
XXVI	Capt. Beloussov presenting the Author with a wedding present from the Russian C-in-C, Gen. Kurasov	203

The photograph on the back of the jacket is taken inside Schönbrunn Palace at a reception given by the British C-in-C, Gen. McCreery. It shows from left to right the Author, Capt. Beloussov, Marshal Koniev, Dr Renner and Gen. McCreery★

★ *Copyright BBC Hulton Picture Library*
† *By Courtesy of the War Office*

1

Arrival in Vienna

The barrier was between us, forbidding entry to the Soviet zone. We glared across it at each other. I was with a small group of British interpreters – part of the so-called 'Advance Party' – heading for Vienna to prepare for the entry of British forces. This was our first sight of Soviet soldiers – scruffy-looking individuals, their slim bodies in faded dirty grey-green uniforms, consisting of a loose tunic with a high collar and wide sleeves, caught in by a leather belt at the waist. Baggy trousers disappeared into high leather boots. The boots were muddy.

The soldiers clutched machine-guns. They scowled at us with pale, drawn faces. They made no move to raise the barrier and the sergeant made no attempt to read the documents which the Major, accompanying us, had handed him; he was presumably illiterate. It was we civilians they kept glancing at as they whispered among themselves. We remained silent while the Major repeated again and again that many civilians had already crossed the frontier.

It was a momentous occasion for me. I was White Russian; those men across the barrier were 'communist murderers'. I felt the strong emotional link of hatred and at the same time an intense curiosity as I stared at them.

My family had escaped from Russia during the revolution in 1917, when I was three. We settled in Britain where I grew up in a close White Russian refugee community centred on our Russian Orthodox church. We were Monarchists, dedicated to the destruction of the Soviet State, guilty of inhuman crimes against the Russian people, and to the restoration of the monarchy in what was for us 'Holy Russia'. We lived by the motto 'For the Tsar, for our Country and our Faith'. Portraits of the Imperial family hung in our rooms. On the anniversary of their assassination, dressed in black we mourned them at a Memorial Service in the Russian church.

Now here I was, a British interpreter, about to enter Soviet-occupied territory. It was 31st July 1945. Austria had been divided into four parts, British, American, French and Soviet, in accordance with the Yalta treaty, each under the control of one of the Allies, Vienna to be governed jointly. The Allied Commission for Austria (ACA) composed of the four Allies was to oversee the government of the whole country.

The sergeant nodded; the barrier was lifted. We left the Semmering Pass and the road zig-zagged steeply down the hill. At each bend a Soviet soldier stood at the salute. They must have expected the General to be in the car. General Winterton, our future Deputy Commander-in-Chief, who headed our Advance Party, had flown into Vienna by plane. We were travelling in his Daimler. Our Major returned the salutes and so we progressed slowly through the Soviet Army ranks. These soldiers with their unsmiling faces and an old-man look about them made us silent and thoughtful. They seemed almost inhuman – that was our first impression.

'I'm glad they are not our enemies!' was the Major's comment.

In the silent, looted devastation caused by the Russians, not the war, through which we now drove, the locals hurried along eyes lowered. Strangely, the children showed no fear; they clustered round the Soviet soldiers lounging in the villages and they clambered all over the odd tank or car being repaired at the side of the road.

We ate our picnic lunch in a field. Large notices in Russian said 'Cleared of Mines'. Food restored our morale. Soviet lorries, crammed with standing troops, rumbled past. One lorry braked and stopped. The soldiers shouted and waved at us. We were alarmed, but it was some time before we understood: 'Mines! Get out of there!' We pointed to the notice, but they only shouted louder. Finally, hardly daring to breathe, we picked our way, stepping lightly, towards the

Arrival in Vienna

road. Nothing happened. The soldiers shouted that their sappers were lazy devils; they stuck up notices without clearing anything; one should never trust them. This later proved correct so we were lucky that time. We did not leave the road again!

As we neared Vienna (BEHA – the Russian notices proclaimed) there were more people to be seen. They looked hungry and dejected, but they smiled and waved to us. Once when we stopped an old man said to us: 'We are waiting for you English and Americans; we don't want the Russians'. Another old man shouted: 'Send us the Duke of Windsor. Let him be our King!' A little boy told us that he was not at school because the Russians had smashed it all up.

At the first check point a young officer asked: 'Any drink?' On hearing, 'No,' he opened the door of the car and stared down at a case of whisky.

'The General's,' the Major explained. Regretfully, the Russian slammed the door shut. At every post soldiers and Austrians stared at the Union Jack in surprise. They had no idea the Allies were on their way in.

At about eight in the evening, we stopped on the outskirts of Vienna to ask the way. While I was waiting by the car a British soldier suddenly appeared and gaped at the flag. I asked who he was and what he was doing there. He told me he had been there for years hiding with the family of his girlfriend. He said it was good to see the Union Jack. He stretched out his hand, almost touching it, but withdrew it quickly saying that he had better not stay around since technically he was a deserter. He vanished as suddenly as he had appeared.

We were directed to the Park Hotel Schönbrunn placed by the Soviets at the disposal of the British Mission. As we entered we heard music and the shuffling noise of many feet; it was coming from a big dance hall still open to the public at the back of the hotel.

In the front part which was to be our private British quarters, the dining-room was full of officers impressive in their smart uniforms and gleaming buttons and buckles; many had the red tabs of a colonel. There was only one civilian – our future British Consul, Mr Williams – who we were told had been sent ahead to contact any Britishers who needed help. His presence was not to be broadcast. He looked out of place in his dark suit. He seemed rather aloof sitting at a table by himself.

We sat down with a group of our officer-interpreters who had arrived a few days before us. The Interpreters' Pool to which our group belonged consisted of a Colonel, a Major, several junior officers and about thirty Russian, German and French-speaking civilian interpreters and translators. I was a Russian interpreter with the substantive rank of major.

The hotel, we were informed, had water though only cold and electricity which worked spasmodically; the city generally had none. Food was brought in by our military, every meal consisting of tinned tea, with milk and sugar already added, and Spam. Locally we could get beer, the water being undrinkable – Russian soldiers bathed regularly in the reservoirs.

Over our tinned tea and Spam we questioned the officers about the Soviets and their behaviour. Yes, they confirmed the horrific stories we had been hearing; they were all too true. Every night from the hotel they heard screams and shots. Drunken soldiers were everywhere. Austrians pleaded with the officers to save them, to get them out of the city. But there was nothing they could do to help.

One Russian-speaking officer suddenly laughed: 'Yes, it's all true. Still, they're likeable rogues really, these Red Army soldiers.' Seeing the protest on the faces around him, he continued: 'They've been so long away from home – five years. They're peasants. They're sick and tired of the war and the sacrifices required of them. And what they are doing now isn't as bad as what the Germans and Austrians did to them and, more importantly, to their families.'

Vienna was still under martial law with a curfew at nine p.m. We were instructed never to go out alone, especially after dark, and first thing in the morning to get ourselves into uniform. Orders were that no Britishers were to be in Vienna out of uniform. I listened and was afraid, but at the same time I was moved by how young these Soviet soldiers were; some of those we had seen could not have been more than sixteen.

We were taken to watch the dancing. The hall was crammed with Soviet officers, distinguished by their stiff epaulettes, and soldiers with their girlfriends, Russian and Austrian, sitting at small tables

Arrival in Vienna

around the heaving mass in the centre. We could hardly push our way in. The Russians were all armed – they were apparently not allowed to go out without arms. Cigarette smoke filled the room. There was a stench of sweat and unwashed bodies, a smell that was to pursue us for the next few months since soap was unobtainable. There were several Russian girls in uniform, mostly traffic wardens, in a loose tunic and skirt with a leather belt. They wore berets. Most of the men were drunk.

We squeezed in at a table. Voices near us were suddenly raised above the din of the music. A young officer sat glaring at his Russian girlfriend. As she shrank from him she shouted: 'Uncivilised!' (We learnt later that this was a terrible insult to any Russian).

He yelled back: 'Traitor!' For a moment they faced each other. Then he continued shouting above the general hubbub: 'You worked for the Germans! I know. You betrayed our country! You thought us barbarians!'

'And so you are!' she screamed back. With a quick gesture seizing his beer bottle, she whirled it through the air and crashed it down on his head. Beer spilled all over him.

He sprang to his feet, groping for his revolver which had slipped round to the back of his belt. As he struggled to reach it several officers tried to grab him. Others began to pull them away, shouting: 'Leave him alone'.

Chairs were pushed back, shots resounded and pandemonium broke loose.

Our officers, with visions of mass shooting in the confined space, rushed out to collect two British Military Policemen on duty outside. They hustled them in and pointing to the struggling mass of legs and arms shouted: 'Get him out!' The MPs, solid, massive creatures, completely indifferent to the uproar, forced their way through the crowd and grabbed the most vociferous individual fighting in the middle of the crush.

There were cries of: 'No! No! That's the Commandant!' The MPs dropped the Commandant and seized the actual culprit by the arms and legs. He struggled violently and bit one of the MPs on the hand while others continued to fight around them.

They edged their way towards the door. When they were outside we did not see what happened, but were told that, to quieten the man, the MPs hit his head against the brick wall to the cheers of the Austrian populace outside. They bundled him into their jeep and drove off to the nearest Commandatura. These local Commandaturas, like police stations, were dotted around all over the place. They all worked under the Soviet Commandant of the first or central district.

We returned to our own side of the hotel, alarmed, but also laughing. The MP who had been bitten came to complain; he was afraid of getting hydrophobia. He was seen off.

Our officers were worried. They had overstepped their rights. Being guests of the Russians they had no authority to bring in the MPs and no responsibility for law and order. Soon enough this was brought home to them. Another Commandant, large and impressively heavy, appeared looking grave and eyed us suspiciously. Our officers apologised and explained that they had been afraid of general shooting breaking out. The Commandant replied that that was all very well, but what was bad was that the Austrians, our common enemy, had witnessed the event. They had jeered at a Russian officer and this officer had been manhandled in public by our MPs. Our officers agreed that it had been a mistake. They offered their sincere apologies. Whereupon drinks were handed round and the Commandant good-naturedly accepted the apology and a glass of whisky.

He stayed drinking and chatting for some time. As he was finally leaving apparently satisfied, he turned round and announced: 'Don't worry about the man. He will be shot,' and he stalked out. We were horrified and went to bed considerably cowed. Weeks later, the same man was seen lounging drunkenly on a bench in a local Commandatura. By that time we had got used to the 'he will be shot' solution of the Russians' problems. In one instance, some of our officers had been insulted by Soviet guards at a frontier post. When they complained they were told the men would be shot. The men were taken behind the shed. There was the sound of machine-gun fire. Our people were considerably distressed until they spotted the men slipping away through the trees.

That night I could not sleep and heard a party of Soviet soldiers passing the hotel swinging along back to barracks from the day's work. They were singing in harmony, a tenor in the lead. There was

Arrival in Vienna

a breadth to the notes and a richness of sound rarely heard. I listened, delighted, until the voices faded in the distance and only the deep basses still hung in the air.

2

A Foreign and Rather Terrifying Atmosphere

It proved impossible to get into uniform as the ATS (Women's Army HQ) produced only one summer shirt to fit me, and Janet, the other girl in our group of interpreters, found nothing to fit her. Janet, a German speaker and our typist, was Scottish, pretty, always cheerful and tolerant of those around her – an ideal companion. We became friends. As we had to remain in civilian clothes and were unable to go out alone, we were taken on a tour of the city in a jeep by Alec, a Russian-speaking Intelligence officer.

Alec was an old friend. We had been up at Oxford together and had kept in touch ever since. He had a kind face, a gentle smile and was most unmilitary-looking. His uniform never looked right on him, he was no athlete and was quite incapable of enforcing any order. At heart he was a pacifist, but his Russian was so good that he had been snatched up by the Intelligence Corps.

As he picked us up, he had a cheerful grin on his face. He told Janet she must learn Russian – it was so easy – a 'sock' in Russian was 'nosock'. The three Russian generals ranged against Napoleon were 'Cut-us-off', 'Knock-him-off' and 'Pop-off' (Kutuzov, Nokimov and Popoff). So easy to remember! He fell silent as he pointed out odd Russian graves marked with red boards headed by the Soviet star, dotted along the roads and even in the centre of Vienna.

Here the buildings were battered, desolate and grim from the bombing and shelling. The dust hung in the air. Gutted upper floors

A Foreign and Rather Terrifying Atmosphere

of buildings were silhouetted against the sky. The people in the streets all looked so old; many of the men were crippled, leaning on crutches or on sticks. Their ashen faces looked desperate with hunger.

Many of the soldiers were drunk and staggered about the streets. But those standing on duty gave a smart salute. The marching troops we met were accompanied by skinny, pale children in Red Army uniform, running alongside the columns. These, Alec told us, had been found abandoned and were picked up as the Red Army advanced across their own German-occupied territory. They would be adopted by the men. Meanwhile they were part of the army and were taken care of by the soldiers who had befriended them.

Everyone was on the scrounge. Many appeared to spend their time picking at the debris, and cigarettes were of great value. That morning, before my bed had been made, I had noticed that my cigarette stumps had disappeared from the ash-tray, though the ash remained. Anyone smoking in the street was followed by groups of locals waiting to pick up the stump. Anyone who stopped was immediately approached for a cigarette and often by people well-dressed and well-spoken.

As we drove back, perhaps to distract us from the depressing sights, Alec started telling us about the orgies they, the officers, had had every night since their arrival when vodka for breakfast had been the rule. We were laughing as we returned to the hotel.

A group of prisoners appeared in our street. Some of our officers took them for Russian soldiers and laughed at their unorthodox and tattered uniforms. Then we noticed that they were preceded by two Russian soldiers with machine-guns, while two others escorted the men on either side and another couple brought up the rear.

'These are Vlassov men,' someone explained, 'Russian deserters and traitors. They fought with the Germans against their own people. They will be shot when they cross into the Soviet zone.'

They passed under our windows, mere skeletons, dragging their feet along wearily, supporting each other. One man collapsed. As his companions tried to raise him, the whole column stumbled to a halt. The soldiers stood waiting for the man to recover.

It is shameful to remember that we turned away from the windows not daring to offer help. We were afraid of the guards and of what

White Among the Reds

the Soviet reaction might be to our interference. But some Red Army men passing stopped and put their hands in their pockets. They brought out whatever they had – cigarettes and sweets – and handed them to the prisoners. We heard one of the guards explaining that there was no provision for feeding the prisoners; they just had to get along as best they could.

As I turned to Alec for comfort, I saw he had gone very pale. His face twitched. He started to say something, then hurried away. He always had shared too deeply the pain of others. Fortunately, I knew he was also quick to share their joy.

We came across such distressing scenes time and again during the next few weeks. They reminded me of the Soviet women patients I had met in the military hospital in Rome. Their husbands had fought with the Germans, one as an officer. They had been expecting repatriation when a priest of the Uniat Church had offered them asylum in Italy. They had refused. I couldn't understand it.

'But you say your husbands will be shot,' I protested.

'Possibly, but who knows? Perhaps not,' a young woman had replied, as she rocked her baby. Then she added: 'It's all so strange here. They're not like us and we don't understand their language.'

'You could learn it,' I suggested.

'I want to go home, to be among our own people, whatever happens,' she replied.

What fatalists, I thought sadly.

Almost immediately we were given a taste of the kind of problem we would have to face in our work. Two American correspondents were arrested by the Russians for photographing Russian officers buying goods on the forbidden Black Market (the Press had been allowed into Vienna the day after us). Their cameras were confiscated. They were later released, after a protest had been lodged, but the film was retained. The *Daily Herald* correspondent was also arrested and locked up for the night for having no pass after curfew; he was released the next morning. The Americans threatened to write up the whole story. We saw nothing strange in the fact that correspondents of an Allied power should ferret out and report on the more shameful

The Author wearing her Union Jack brooch.

General Rogov and orphan adopted at Stalingrad.

White Among the Reds

aspects of Russian occupation. We found it shocking that the Press should be molested in any way.

The Russians found the incidents amusing and hoped it would teach the correspondents a lesson. We were still under martial law and it was prohibited to photograph Russian troops.

At about the same time a Russian officer phoned accusing us British of holding up at our frontier a coal train much needed in Vienna. It turned out that it was they themselves who were holding it up. When everything was finally straightened out, the Russian on the phone remarked: 'We seem to take turns at holding things up, don't we?' Such incidents were inevitable in his eyes.

I watched our Russian-speaking officers sorting out these incidents and wondered whether I would be able to cope on my own.

Vienna night life consisted in driving through the streets at great speed to avoid military patrols and groups of drunken soldiers, and going to the Opera, still miraculously functioning, though not in the Opera House, which had been destroyed.

I went there with a group of officers from our zone. The theatre was crammed. People were standing in the aisles. The audience stared at the foreign uniforms. It was the first inkling they had that British troops were arriving. And what a contrast they presented to the dishevelled, sulky-looking Russian soldiers filling the theatre! I watched these soldiers with interest. They seemed to be treating the locals as they treated each other; some were rough, uncouth types, others were polite and considerate. The Austrians had little to complain of here, I thought.

During the interval we went out for a smoke. We were immediately surrounded by an Austrian crowd of stump collectors. As each of us threw down a cigarette stump, someone sprang forward to pick it out of the mud.

As we left one of our officers fell back. I looked round to see what had delayed him. He was standing there, so tall, in his smart uniform, and with a great bristly moustache, holding the door open for a one-legged scruffy-looking Austrian, whom his companions were ignoring and who was unable to open the door himself.

A Foreign and Rather Terrifying Atmosphere

The second evening we went to the Opera was with a Brigadier from the provinces. We saw *Tosca* with Ivanov, the baritone from Moscow. He sang in Russian, the Austrians in German. It was magnificent singing, but when Ivanov chased the heroine round the stage, there were titters in the audience. It was a too familiar sight, seeing a Russian chasing an Austrian girl. Yet when it was over and Ivanov bent over the heroine's hand and kissed it, there was tumultuous applause.

In the interval when we approached a group of Russians they nudged each other and formed a friendly circle around us. They became very witty at our expense; they did not realise some of us spoke Russian. We were approached by a group of senior Russian officers, among whom was a woman major, with three 'wound' stripes on the sleeve of her uniform. She was a broad, solid female, who flung her weight about and spoke louder than the men. The Russians round us backed away. But our Brigadier took her on and enquired through Alec whether she was enjoying the Opera.

'Yes, yes. It is good,' she replied.

The Brigadier went on: 'What exactly is the story? I don't seem able to make head or tail of it.'

The woman major was shocked. 'The story! And you coming from Rome! You mean to say that at your age you do not know the story of *Tosca*!' She went on berating him while he edged away and the Russians grinned. She had apparently commanded a fighting unit of men and 'They must have been terrified of her,' added the Russian who told me this.

Once we were entertained by our hosts, the Red Army. We were invited to a 'Concert' consisting of classical music and ballet, which included the Leningrad dancer, Ulanova. Our small group were the only non-Russians there. I got a different impression of them. The men were fairly smart and orderly. They lacked polish, but they seemed pleasant enough. We sat behind a group of Russian generals – all pot-bellied, with almost shaven heads. Before and during the interval they strutted around, smoking their long cigarettes. One general looked like a huge gorilla with a terrifying scowl. Behind us sat the more junior officers and right at the back the soldiers.

The applause was adequate but not enthusiastic. The Red Army did not appreciate ballet, however good, nor classical music. But in the last dance Ulanova appeared in what has come to be known as a 'see-through' top. I saw the two generals sitting in front of me nudging each other and smiling coyly. One whispered to the other: 'Good thing the wife's not here!' At the end the hall rang out with applause and shouts of 'Bis! Bis!' (The Russian equivalent of 'Encore'). Ulanova danced again. It was surprising that no one had warned her not to appear like that before an army audience.

A Colonel Rich sitting beside me kept fidgeting, glancing round the hall and whispering: 'Most extraordinary! What an extraordinary situation!'

We were introduced to our working quarters in the Schönbrunn Palace – an ornate reception room, complete with chandeliers, gilded mirrors, walls and doors with decorative panels, and red plush chairs. There my friend, Janet, and I were photographed for the Press as being the first two civilian women to arrive in Vienna.

While we sorted out our things, our sergeant-intepreter started typing Pushkin's poems. He wanted to practise his Russian.

In strolled a Soviet officer. He had a broad, attractive face, with a child-like pink and white complexion, blue eyes, a high forehead and curly fair hair. As with most Russians, he held himself very straight. His stiff epaulettes stuck out squarely over his shoulders; they were the only aggressive thing about him.

He walked casually towards the sergeant and looked over his shoulder. Then he started reading a poem aloud with great feeling. Suddenly he exclaimed: 'You've made spelling mistakes! Look what you've written!' He proceeded to correct the sergeant's spelling and reproved him for not looking up the words in the dictionary!

We enquired who he might be. He introduced himself as Major Kovalev, liaison officer between the two Commanders-in-Chief, Marshal Koniev and Lieutenant-General McCreery. We shook hands. We asked him whether he spoke English. He looked embarrassed and admitted that he knew only a few words such as 'OK', but he was an educated man, he had been a school-teacher in civilian life and he was sure we would get along easily together. We took this seriously

A Foreign and Rather Terrifying Atmosphere

as it was obvious to us even then that, charming though he was, Major Kovalev had little sense of humour. He spent the rest of the morning initiating the sergeant into Russian literature.

People were coming and going around us, bringing documents. They were astonished at this Russian officer, standing relaxed in the middle of the room reciting poetry.

Later, he himself was to bring us numerous documents from his C-in-C, usually marked 'Immediate' or 'Urgent'. They were in Russian and had to be translated into English. He found us Russian-speakers (we usually moved in a group as it was thus easier to deal with any problem that arose) whatever the time of day or evening, and wherever we happened to be. He appeared in our midst whether we were in our hotel, or with friends, or merely walking in the park. In the middle of a party, there he was, a document in one hand, and a bottle in the other. He soon learnt that the bottle always made him welcome. We repeatedly asked him how he managed to track us down; he just shrugged and changed the subject. Presumably he was informed by their Secret Service, who must have kept a constant eye on our movements.

The first time he appeared with one such document, we were in the dining-room of the Park Hotel Schönbrunn. (It now displayed a notice saying 'British Officers' Transit Hotel'). I had been saying that most Russians were natural singers, when in he walked.

'Do you sing?' an American colleague, Charlie Thayer, asked him. (Charlie was Alec's cousin and shared his irrepressible sense of humour). Kovalev opened his mouth and sang. He had a pleasant tenor and no self-consciousness. Charlie took us all to a private room upstairs so as not to cause a riot in the public dining-room!

Another time when he made an unexpected appearance at a party, Kovalev was greeted with cries of 'Speech! Speech!' Always courteous and obliging, protesting only mildly, he climbed on to the chair offered him and began: 'The Soviet Union is the greatest country in the world (appreciative grunts of applause). We have the highest standard of living and we are first in the field of education (applause). We are first in most spheres of activity,' and so on. A typically Soviet appraisal. As he continued, the applause became boisterous; it was some time before Kovalev realised that his speech was appreciated but for the wrong reasons. He got down off the chair, embarrassed and offended, murmuring that he never could understand our sense of humour. He had a literal mind and took things seriously.

But with his unassuming manner and obvious sincerity Kovalev helped considerably to make us feel more at home in this foreign and rather terrifying atmosphere and for myself, I now felt ready and eager to get down to work.

So few were we Russian speakers that after the first few days I found myself, inexperienced as I was, coping with whatever had to be done on my own.

Translations were crowding in upon us. They were relatively easy; we had dictionaries covering most subjects and between us all in the office, we had specialised knowledge on most aspects of military life and problems of 'occupation'.

Documents had to be translated from Russian into English. Our documents were submitted to the Russians in English and their translators put them into Russian.

Russian documents conformed to no grammar or dictionary. We had to make sense of their notes, and often to concoct reasonable texts from garbled verbal messages. One also had to be careful to convey the feeling behind the words. Mistakes could misrepresent the state of Allied relations. General Winterton, Head of our Advance Party and British Deputy C-in-C, was delighted to receive a letter from a Russian general couched, to his surprise, considering the strained relations between them, in the most affectionate terms. It had come in reply to a letter of Winterton's beginning 'Dear General'. The word 'Dear' had been taken literally by the Russian translators and rendered as a term of endearment! No harm done in this case, but it was a warning of how careful one should be.

Our translations were circulated by us to our Allies, the French and Americans. Charlie Thayer, who was from the State Department, was acting interpreter for the American Deputy C-in-C, General Gruenther, and De Becque was doing the same for the French General, Cherrière. We had become friends and worked as a group.

It was the speed at which these documents had to be translated that

A Foreign and Rather Terrifying Atmosphere

was taxing. Sometimes Russian documents arrived at the Hotel late in the evening. These had to be translated, typed and delivered as soon as ready so that General Winterton should be able to study them over his breakfast.

I had to work through the night when the heating went off and the city became silent. Everyone slept. I was no typist so when the translation was finished I had to wake Janet. Without a protest she climbed out of bed and sat down to work, shivering with sleepiness and cold, my fur coat over her night clothes. I dozed while she typed a page and woke to give her the next.

The document finished, it still had to be delivered. As we civilians had not been issued with passes or uniforms, I was afraid of being stopped and even shot at by Russian night patrols – they carried machine-guns. When I once protested about travelling alone at night, I was advised by an officer: 'If challenged, always stop. And if they open the car door, just bark "General!" at them and they'll let you through. They're terrified of generals.'

It sounded absurd, but once when I was challenged and stopped, as soon as the car door swung open, automatically I shouted: 'General!' Immediately the door was slammed shut, my driver, as scared as myself, took off rapidly and behind us we heard the soldiers firing into the air.

3

Russian Obstruction?

The first time I was sent to the Russian central Commandatura was to protest about a train the Russians were holding up at their frontier outside the city. It was carrying Austrian civilians, mostly children. There was no food or water. Permission for this train to enter Vienna had been given by the Soviet authorities. My instructions were to get hold of the Commandant and tell him what had happened.

A jeep with a soldier at the wheel took me to the Commandatura. An enormous Soviet flag flew menacingly over the area, while massive portraits of Lenin and Stalin glared down at the crowds below. Outside Soviet sentries stood with fixed bayonets. I got out of the jeep, wondering how I should proceed. The sentries stared motionlessly ahead. I hesitated wondering whether they were there to stop people passing or just for show. They looked forbidding.

Finally I approached a sentry and asked: 'Is one allowed in?'

He mumbled: 'I don't know,' without looking at me.

'But will you let me pass?'

'I don't know.'

I tackled him again: 'If I go past you what will you do?'

He turned a boyish face red with embarrassment towards me and mumbled: 'I don't know anything.' Quickly I slipped past him. Nothing happened.

Inside a passage led into a large hall in the corner of which a Russian officer sat behind a desk. Austrian men and women sat on

Russian Obstruction?

benches all round the walls. The officer was a smart young man, fair-haired and blue-eyed. He smiled easily and greeted everyone politely. I joined the queue of those approaching him and watched him directing each person to the next place on the benches. When my turn came, I said I was from the British forces and wished to see the Commandant.

'Certainly,' said the officer. 'Take a seat. I will see what can be done.' I sat down and waited. More and more people arrived (presumably braving the sentries outside) and took their places on the benches. It was strange to watch this young Russian officer dealing so ably with the problems of these Austrians, who looked as though they belonged to the professional classes. I wondered whether the Austrians despised the Russians as being of an inferior race, as much as the Germans had done.

Another door opened. A slight, grey-haired, distinguished-looking gentleman with pince-nez entered the room. He was dressed in a high-collared white tunic, military trousers with a red stripe down the sides and high leather boots. Escorted by several officers, he started walking round the room. As he approached each person rose, shook hands and sat down again. When he reached me, I also shook hands, wondering who he was and why he was greeting us. Then he left and once again we waited.

Finally I decided that I had sat there long enough. I asked the officer when I could see the Commandant.

'You have seen him,' he replied. 'You shook hands with him.'

I was taken aback, annoyed. 'I must see him again,' I insisted. 'I did not realise who he was.' (I did not confess that I had expected a tougher-looking individual). 'It is very important. Please help me.'

He thought a moment and came up with: 'Why don't you look for him yourself, upstairs?' In no time I was out of the room and up the stairs. On the landing above a group of officers were deep in discussion. In their midst was the Commandant, General Blagodatov.

I walked up, murmuring: 'Excuse me, Mr General. Could I speak to you for a moment?' (The Russians used the term 'Comrade General'. We had been instructed to replace the 'Comrade' wherever it occurred with 'Mr').

He assured me that he would see to it immediately and that the train would be allowed to proceed. I thanked him and after we had all bowed to each other I withdrew down the stairs and out past the same sentries. It was all very strange; at times the Russians treated us almost as enemies and now, here, as one of themselves. The Commandant kept his word; the train was allowed to proceed.

Such incidents were quickly cleared up once we managed to contact a senior Russian officer, but they cropped up continually, disorganising our carefully-laid plans. British military vehicles were halted, our food convoys pilfered, our documents lost.

As far as we interpreters could judge, the incidents arose from inefficiency and stupidity. The Soviet Commandant explained time and again that anything foreign had had to be treated with suspicion automatically for so many years that now junior Soviet officers could not understand why British vehicles must be allowed to pass.

One of his officers went further. 'You see,' he explained, 'these officers at the check points, they can't read the orders. They're newly risen from the ranks. So many were killed. . .'

The Soviet Command dismissed these incidents as trivial; they had to cope with immeasurably more serious problems.

We met a Polish-born British soldier who had been allowed to leave his unit in order to try and find his family in Poland. On his return he dropped in to tell us of his adventures. He had worn British uniform and was on horse-back. The first night behind the Soviet front-line he was seized by Soviet soldiers and locked up. Only in the morning did a Polish-speaker apologise and explain that this had been done on the order of the commanding officer to ensure that during the night he did not fall into the hands of gangs of deserters and brigands who controlled whole areas behind the Soviet front-line. He described the situation there as 'chaotic.'

But our people took the incidents seriously. They began talking of Russian obstruction; they believed it was the result of deliberate policy on the part of the Soviet authorities. And our Press at home splashed the incidents over their front pages and made the most of them. Friction built up rapidly between the Western Allies and the Russians; there were rumours of real trouble breaking out at any moment.

Austrian tales of horrors committed by the Russian soldiers did not help matters. We were appalled at what we heard; nothing and no-one was apparently safe and the Austrians kept begging us to move in quickly to protect them.

Our future Interpreters' Mess suffered at the hands of the Russians. The house was spacious and stood in pleasant gardens but inside it was now filthy, derelict, and badly needed disinfecting. The Interpreters' Mess Officer, who had told us stories of Russian vandalism, had himself been well and truly caught out.

One night when he was on the premises Russian officers appeared and asked whether they might pass the night there; they had come a long way, were very tired, and had nowhere to go. Knowing this was often true – that the Russians were normally expected to make their own way – and seeing that these were Guards officers, he reluctantly agreed and left them bedding down for the night on the floor. There was scant furniture, anyway, but there were some valuable leather chairs and a leather settee. The walls also were covered in leather.

When the officer returned in the morning the Russians had moved on and so had all the leather off the furniture and even off the walls, and the place was filthy. He was very angry. Whenever we pulled his leg about it, he repeated indignantly: 'But they were Guards officers!'

Two Russians drove up to the caretaker's house. While he was away for only three minutes they managed to collect all his and his wife's belongings and were gone by the time he returned.

In the evenings as we foregathered in the hotel, our officer-interpreters were called out to deal with incidents several times every night. One 'Hero of the Soviet Union' who was drunk, parked his car on the site reserved for General Winterton. It was with difficulty that he was persuaded to go elsewhere. Another Soviet officer tried to drive into the Schönbrunn Park. He was stopped by a sentry who called for an interpreter. An ATS officer went to his help and agreed to escort the Russian through the Park. She was seen disappearing into the trees with him and a brute of a chauffeur behind. One of our officers hurried after them and turned angrily on the Russian who replied that the girl had come of her own volition so he thought her fair game.

Austrian girls leaving the Russians for British soldiers caused most of the trouble. The Russians were jealous and angry though none of the Allies were supposed to 'fraternise'; that is, to have any social contact with the Austrians. One British soldier out with an Austrian girl was stopped by a Russian officer. He ran away. The officer struck the girl with his revolver and took a shot at her, wounding her face. However, two other Russians came to her rescue.

An Intelligence officer, out in his car with a girl, was stopped by a Soviet officer asking for a lift. But once inside the Russian drew his revolver, forced the Britisher out of the car and went off with the girl and the car.

As these tales of our own clashes with the Russians and the Austrian horror stories poured in, were mulled over, repeated and exaggerated in the telling, they stifled all other considerations and the ordinary Russian soldier assumed the aspect of some kind of monster. British soldiers began to look down on the Russians and tried to keep out of their way as much as possible, while the Russians, taken aback by so much opprobrium, developed a dangerous inferiority complex. They began to avoid any unnecessary contact with their Allies. They began to keep themselves to themselves.

At first our officers had been invited into the Russian Officers' Mess. Manners were primitive; officers got drunk and were sick in public. The Britishers must have shown their disgust; they were never asked again, nor were further invitations issued to anyone except to official functions.

Only once did one of our senior officers come up against the NKVD troops, as the KGB were then called. They were the real toughs. He found them installed in a house allotted to us. They would not allow him to pass. He forced his way in shouting at the top of his voice. To his surprise they scattered.

But there were Russian officers, probably from the NKVD, speaking quite good English, whom we never met officially but who mingled with Western officers and tried to get them to open up and say what they thought of the Soviet regime. One such individual criticised the Soviet Union and tried to draw us out to do the same. Later I saw him talking to a group of our soldiers, telling them that Jews held the best positions in the Soviet Union; he was probing to see whether British soldiers also thought along these Nazi lines. Our

Russian Obstruction?

soldiers nodded their heads in agreement with whatever he said; they did not care who held what posts in the Soviet Union. These agents-provocateurs must have relayed very misleading reports about the views of our military.

It was against this troubled background that the Allies began holding quadrupartite meetings planning the Western Allies' entry into Vienna, setting up the organs of the Allied Commission for Austria and dealing with current problems. The ACA was to be a military affair consisting of four Allied Commanders-in-Chief and four Deputy C-in-Cs who would preside over the highest organs of the Commission, the Allied Council and its Executive Committee respectively. Under these came the special quadrupartite Committees or Divisions staffed by military or civilian specialists dealing with internal affairs, economic matters, displaced persons and so forth.

I started interpreting first for a Brigadier Verney, who was to head the Internal Affairs Division. He was an impressive officer, well-groomed, slim and with sleek black hair. I drove down to meetings with him in his gleaming official car, flag flying, police and soldiers saluting and the populace gaping as we swept past.

At meetings I sat beside him and translated his words into Russian, taking them either sentence by sentence or, as seemed more sensible, paragraph by paragraph, whichever he preferred. The Brigadier stopped speaking when he wished to be translated. It was remarkable how quickly one acquired the knack. Though I was nervous at the beginning I was soon able to carry a short speech in my head, with the aid of just a few notes – odd words – to indicate the sequence of what had been said. One strange discovery was that, the translating finished, I found I no longer remembered what had been said. If I was interrupted, the same thing happened. I had no memory of what had gone before. Brigadier Verney was very considerate; he was presumably also doing this kind of work for the first time. At first the atmosphere was tense; we were all nervous.

My first two meetings went smoothly enough. At the first, the Russian delegates were a Colonel Ilichev, a slight figure with grey hair cut short, a greyish face and small darting eyes, who always sat still and spoke rarely, and his deputy, Lieutenant-Colonel Miasnikov, a suspicious-looking character, with heavy-lidded eyes, dark rounded eyebrows, a long morose-looking face and a balding scalp. He glanced at you and then quickly withdrew his gaze. Both had green bands round their caps indicating that they belonged to the frontier guards. They appeared without an interpreter.

I found myself doing the introductions and explaining to each side who was who and what Brigadier Verney as Chairman proposed to discuss. The Russians then asked me to interpret for them also. At future meetings they continued to come without an interpreter and soon it was taken for granted that at these meetings I would do all the Anglo-Russian interpreting.

At the first meeting of the Chiefs of Staff there were a whole series of set-backs. Our General Packard, who was particular about his appearance, slit his trousers on a nail. I had to pin him up with a safety pin. I had a dreadful cold and as General Packard was presiding I had to do most of the talking. Finally I choked; I could not stop coughing. General Packard slapped me on the back and plied me with water till I was able to continue, but only in a husky whisper.

The Russian delegate, General Morozov, their Chief of Staff, then spoke at great length. This gave me a break, in which to recover. He had brought a young officer as interpreter who kept his head down and darted nervous glances at us foreigners. He now mumbled a few words, fell silent and then added hurriedly: 'The General doesn't like your arrangements. They're no good.' And that was all. General Packard flared up with irritation at so abrupt a criticism. I explained the misinterpretation. After several such unfortunate instances General Morozov asked me to interpret for him too.

I glanced at the young officer; he gave me a smile of relief, so I took over. He was probably an ADC with a smattering of English. I did my best between coughs, being slapped on the back and drinking water. I had to struggle on for three hours.

When it was all over, General Morozov thanked me profusely and said that they would have to carry me off to work for them. As he drove away, Russian style, amidst a cavalcade of cars, I hoped he did not mean it literally.

The next time I appeared to interpret for General Packard there was a large jug of water and a glass all ready for me.

At the meetings which followed the Russians often failed to turn up, or else came late, without the documents they needed. Sometimes they came totally unbriefed, so before the meeting could start I had to explain to them the questions on the agenda.

At a meeting of Economists, a Russian colonel, also without an interpreter, faced three highly qualified Allied economists. It was obvious that he knew nothing about economics. He sweated away, repeating over and over again: 'I have no information.' Our delegate did not seem to realise that this was strictly true. He pressed him hard and asked him whether he had received instructions according to Stalin's promise at Potsdam that the Red Army would feed Vienna. The Russian varied his reply by saying that he knew nothing about it, that no mention had been made in the Press – again strictly true, but not to the point and most unsatisfactory for the Western delegates.

Much later, when I got to know Colonel Miasnikov of the Internal Affairs Division better, he admitted that he had been sent to a financial meeting though he knew nothing about finances because at the time, there was no-one else. So perforce he had had nothing to contribute and could only 'stick it out'. He was unable even to report anything back to his own people, since he had not understood what had been discussed.

It seemed that the Russians were not yet ready for such meetings. Their specialists, if they existed, were not yet available. But they were determined not to admit this or anything else that our Press might seize on to make them look either ridiculous or deliberately obstructive. They took refuge in silence.

Our people, ready for action, were frustrated. This started the legend of the Russians being 'inscrutable'.

I then realised how difficult it is, when there is no common language, to establish any kind of relationship and how mysterious perfectly ordinary people can appear to each other. Interpreting, as I came to see it, involved not only translating words but also creating an atmosphere which would help to establish relationships and understanding between the delegates.

On August 15th, I was invited to a banquet given by General Cherrière, the French Deputy Commander-in-Chief. It was to be a great occasion, to celebrate the capitulation of the Japanese, to eat a

White Among the Reds

chamois which he had shot and to bring together those Allied generals who were already in Vienna.

Russian generals would be present De Becque, the French liaison officer, told me and would I please entertain them.

This plunged me into a quandary. It would be the first time that I would be meeting Soviets – that is, communists – socially. This I had not foreseen. It was one thing meeting Soviet officers in the course of duty but quite another associating with them on a friendly basis. I was worried; I did not quite know how to handle the situation.

We drove up to the Kümmer Hotel, our officer-interpreters and I. This was the French HQ. The barrier in front was painted in French national colours, red, white and blue; a Moroccan guard of honour stood statue-like in white turbans. The crowds jostled to get a glimpse of what was going on.

The guests were first offered cocktails while the Moroccan band, their goat mascot at their head, played outside in the courtyard. The American Commandant, General Lewis was there, Brigadier Palmer, our Commandant, General Morozov, the Russian Chief of Staff, and General Blagodatov, the Russian Commandant. General Winterton, whom I was seeing for the first time, came in last. He strode in, tall, handsome, elegant and, I was later to learn, spirited, sensitive and sometimes mischief-making, like a spoilt youngster. He obviously enjoyed making an entrance and was conscious of admiring glances.

We had by this time been issued with ACA badges – the letters ACA over the Eighth Army sign. I wore this badge prominently since I was disobeying Standing Orders, though unintentionally, by not wearing uniform. General Winterton was delighted with the badge – he had designed it himself. He led me around showing it off to all and sundry.

We went in to dinner. The long table looked magnificent with the four Allied flags, the four menus in national colours and red, white and yellow roses cascading down the length of the table. I found myself seated in the centre next to General Morozov, the Russian Chief of Staff, and opposite General Blagodatov, the Russian Commandant. Morozov was square-headed and square-jawed; a broad, short individual; he scowled and appeared tough. Blagodatov could be taken for a professional man with soft, white, well-groomed hands.

Russian Obstruction?

For some time we three sat in silence amidst the general hubbub, staring down at our plates. These I had been brought up to consider as Reds, communist murderers, who had destroyed everything my family cherished. I was, however, conscious of the fact that to them I represented a bourgeois, capitalist society, the exploiters of the peasants and workers. I was confused and embarrassed.

General Morozov leant forward and picked a red rose from the centrepiece on the table. He handed it to me, saying: 'Perhaps it is best said with a flower?' I took the rose. Morozov smiled. Unexpectedly, his face lit up in the friendliest manner. I picked a white rose and handed it to him.

'White is not for me,' he said. 'White stands for innocence. You can give it to him,' indicating General Blagodatov. 'He is pure; he neither smokes nor drinks, and he doesn't chase women – though he doesn't object to being chased! No, I am a sinful man.'

'You can give him a yellow rose,' General Blagodatov chimed in. 'Yellow stands for unfaithfulness. . .' He got a scowl from his colleague.

The gulf between us having been bridged, they plied me with questions. They already knew my name. I had a revolutionary great-grandfather, Ivan Poustchine, whom they revered. Now they wanted to know where I lived, what I did, what my family had done on leaving Russia and whether they had managed to succeed in any career, despite their penniless refugee status. I found myself pouring it all out. I was no longer nervous; difficult ethical questions retreated into the background. These men had become pleasant human beings; I could no longer consider them merely as officials of a communist state.

Champagne and cognac flowed. Everyone drank a considerable amount and talked more freely. There were numerous speeches. Our senior officers stammered through the interpretations as best they could for they too had drunk heavily. Most of the speeches were conciliatory and optimistic. They dealt with such generalities as 'Successful future co-operation after successful co-operation in war.'

Now and then formal speech was abandoned. The Generals began sniping at each other.

White Among the Reds

General Winterton sighed saying that: 'At last the war is over. There will be no more fighting!'

To which General Morozov countered: 'And tomorrow the paper battle begins!'

Winterton flared up: 'But I hate paper as much as you.'

Morozov: 'I had not noticed it.' He was referring to the deluge of complaints he was receiving from us.

After dinner there was dancing. The atmosphere was heated, intimate; few remained sober. In between dances I escaped from the clutching hands of rather drunken French colonels and went to the aid of the Russians.

Both Russian generals kept off controversial subjects. They never mentioned Stalin or communism. They might equally well have been First World War generals. But General Winterton repeatedly cornered them; he tried to catch them out on some disputed point; he refused to take his mind off work. While he was talking to one of the Russians the French hostess pranced up to him and invited him to dance. She was offended when he replied: 'Work before pleasure.'

To ease the atmosphere our host threatened forfeits for anyone talking shop. I immediately demanded a forfeit off General Winterton. As he good-naturedly downed his champagne, I found myself singing with Blagodatov 'Pei do dna!' (Bottoms up). As another forfeit off him Cherrière demanded a ball in Schönbrunn Palace at the New Year. Winterton enquired of Blagodatov whether he would consider coming to such a ball? Blagodatov replied that though he was Commandant of the city he had never been invited to the Schönbrunn Palace. Winterton hastened to assure him that as soon as the Palace was repaired he would receive an invitation.

Cherrière asked Blagodatov why he had to display such enormous pictures of Lenin and Stalin on the Soviet Commandatura; they hit the eye for miles around.

'Exactly! That is their purpose,' Blagodatov replied calmly. 'So that everyone can see that it is the Commandatura for miles around.'

When Blagodatov had to pay a forfeit, Winterton, in an attempt to embarrass him shouted to me: 'Kiss him! Kiss him!' I had to withdraw quickly and pretend not to have heard.

The American, General Lewis, remarked to Morozov: 'You don't look right in your job. You look too much of a soldier to care for civilians and to take up politics.'

'But war is the result of politics,' Morozov answered. 'Surely we soldiers who have had the same experiences and are therefore better able to understand each other, shouldn't we find it easier to make a better job of politics?'

There was this undercurrent of sparring, West and East against each other, which would always be present on social occasions.

At midnight General Morozov proposed the toast: 'To victory and everlasting peace!' Together we all raised our glasses.

4

Everything Suspended

The work of our Advance Party was completed. Most of the British element of the Commission had arrived. All was set for the Western Allied forces to make their formal entry into Vienna, and for the Allied Commission for Austria to start governing the country. But with the war in the Far East concluded in such an awesome manner, it was in the shadow of the atom bomb that the ACA was to begin its work.

The atom bomb dominated everyone's thoughts. Some people thought its discovery would put an end to war, since war would presumably mean the end of the world. The head of the Secretariat expressed a widely held view that having the atom bomb we Westerners need no longer consider the Russians, their point of view or their intentions; they were no longer of any consequence.

Whatever their attitude to the bomb, most people in the Commission seemed to view the future with intense gloom. At home there was post-war drabness, with food and clothes rationing and uncertainty about future employment; abroad, widespread Allied dissension, and, among the military, actual fear of once again having to shoulder the responsibilities back home: all this, coupled with the knowledge that we now had to live with the bomb, caused general depression.

I kept remembering the horrors that we had foreseen for the years through which we were then living; we had expected civil wars,

Everything Suspended

widespread epidemics, famine, if not actual death. For us none of these horrors had materialised. As a Foreign Office friend quoted: 'To-day is the tomorrow I dreaded so much yesterday and thank God all is well.'

I was also cheered by the attitude of Popski (of Popski's Private Army); he was officially supposed to be our C-in-C's special liasion officer with the Russians. He maintained: 'The quality of life is now better than ever, because though many people are hungry and miserable they are alive. They have come out of the slough. They no longer think that money is everything; they take pleasure in living itself, which they did not do before the war.' And he would repeat: 'People are leading real lives; their problems are real. Everything they do is worth doing.' Such were his views and with the champagne he produced accompanying them, we were eager listeners.

But it was in a general atmosphere of gloom and depression that the ACA was supposed to start functioning. There was trouble from the start and at the highest level. The meeting of the C-in-Cs, which was to herald the entry of our troops and the official start of the Commission's work, was repeatedly delayed. We did not know the reasons, but we felt the tension. First Marshal Koniev, the Soviet C-in-C, then General McCreery, our C-in-C, refused each other's proposed dates for the Allied Council meeting. Everything was suspended, and we waited.

Taking advantage of the lull in activity, the Allies began to settle into their own zones and to organise some sort of normal living.

We had started to mix. The Park Hotel dance hall, now patrolled by our military, was frequented by both British and Russian troops, even though they still chose partners only from among their own nationals or the Austrians. The soldiers in the streets began to get along on some kind of German. Sometimes, when we passed Russian officers, they smiled and said: 'Good-day!' – the sum total of their English.

The Russians completed their withdrawal from our sector and disappeared into their own, which meant that gradually they ceased to appear in the dance hall. Within the city precincts we were allowed to move about freely in each other's zones, but we had to live in our own.

White Among the Reds

Janet and I were left temporarily in the Park Hotel, as it was considered safest. Our NAAFI arrived for the first time, so we had cigarettes, chocolate, whisky and soap, which we sometimes exchanged for wine with Russian officers who would appear in the hotel. Food improved daily; occasionally we even had meat. All food was requisitioned by the army in the provinces. The first time that bread appeared on the table, we pounced on it as though it were the greatest luxury and, dividing it equally, ate it all up then and there. A bar was opened in the hotel. It immediately acquired the atmosphere of an English Officers' Mess, with elegant types lounging around and everyone dropping in for a drink and a gossip. Mr Williams, the Consul, was also to be met there. Tall and handsome, with short, fair curly hair he managed to hold his own against the attraction of the military. Since we girls were unable to get uniforms, he had arranged for one of the ladies of the local British community to embroider Union Jack brooches for us to wear. The Russians were supposed to recognise them and to treat us as Allies. The brooches were better than nothing, though even our officers in British uniform did not appear to be very safe. They looked foreign to the Russian soldiers, who gaped belligerently at them. Knowledge of what was going on and of the fact that Allies were already in Vienna had not permeated to the lower ranks of the Red Army.

Our menfolk were moved out of the Park Hotel and into billets in the Hietzing district of Vienna (the British zone). One officer acquired a superb bed-sitting room at the top of a house. It was circular with windows all the way round, commanding distant views of the city. A huge bed, almost square, stood in the centre amidst palm trees. Such a palatial room cried out for a party. We all foregathered. Many of the guests had already been celebrating the end of the war for the past few days. They were pretty drunk on arrival.

Towards morning there came the usual call to cope with another trainload, this time of children returning to Vienna, travelling in primitive conditions, and now stranded at the Russian frontier. Major Kovalev, the Russian liaison officer, was with us.

When the problem was put to him, he said gaily: 'Just phone our Chief of Staff. He will straighten it out.' We trooped back to the hotel, where there was a telephone. There, we realised the late hour

Everything Suspended

– 2 a.m. But Kovalev assured us that the General would not mind; the phone was at his bedside. It would be quite all right, and he produced the number. When we got through, and a hoarse and furious voice bellowed: 'Who's that?' down the phone, Kovalev fled. Our senior officer had to cope with the irate general. How dare he wake him? Who did he think he was? and so on for quite a time, till finally he calmed down and agreed grudgingly to deal with the problem. The next day the train reached Vienna.

So far, at work, we had all got along in a free and easy and friendly manner, but now that the Secretariat had arrived all the red tape of a government institution descended on our heads. The Interpreters' Pool came directly under the Secretariat.

The senior officer of our Interpreters' Pool was summoned by the Russian Chief of Staff and told that, firstly, Marshal Koniev wanted a meeting of the C-in-Cs on August 14th, and secondly, that Koniev wanted the Austrian government, as set up by them, to extend its influence over the whole of Austria, as a central administrative organ to facilitate the functioning of the economic life of the country. Our officer took notes as he had always done previously and brought them to us; we composed an English text and submitted it to the newly set up Secretariat for distribution. We could no longer hand documents straight to the General's staff.

The Secretariat asked whether our text was a verbatim translation. They insisted that it should be so. Useless to tell them that there was no document to translate, that the Russian General normally expressed himself verbally. They could not conceive of such a thing. Finally we concocted a Russian text, translated it verbatim and passed them this document. Even then they were not satisfied and criticised our translation of what they called the 'original' text. Our corrected document was then circulated to the French and the Americans, together with the British comment. The Secretariat then added an amendment to the comment and finally an amendment to their own amendment. De Becque, the French liaison officer, came hurriedly over to complain and ask what we were playing at. We explained. He accused the Secretariat of picking holes, complicating matters and drawing out proceedings. His General would have to support the British view, he said, out of principle but under protest. This was a

White Among the Reds

taste of things to come. We sometimes felt that our own people could be quite as impossible as the Russians.

Our Western allies were also arriving in greater numbers. American negro mine-clearing units came first. Immediately the Austrian girls left our soldiers and would be seen hanging on to American arms – to the disgust of the British soldiers and the malicious satisfaction of the Russians. The girls knew where food was more plentiful.

One Sunday we managed to organise an excursion into the hills. We were not allowed outside Vienna itself, but the Wiener Wald was within the city precincts. We drove up to the top. We could now view the entire city with the Danube winding its way into the distance. As we stood there we were enveloped in the heady smell of pine. On the summit the walls of an empty hotel were covered with scrawls in Russian.

'Petrov was here!'

'Ivanov was here!'

'Here we are in Vienna, but the Germans never got to Moscow and never will!' – the Red Army immortalising itself.

A group of Russians arrived. They pointed out to each other where their names were inscribed. Two Red Army girls inspected our officers, who were looking particularly smart.

One said: 'Nice fellows. If I were a few years younger, I wouldn't mind. . .'

'Be quiet!' the other, noticing that the officers were smiling, whispered. 'They all understand everything.'

The first one retorted: 'Well, and so what?'

Another Sunday, our new Colonel, appointed to take charge of the Interpreters' Pool (officers from fighting units were being rapidly demobbed and replaced by specialists), invited a number of us to drive up the Kahlenberg. It was a lovely day. We drove through the Weiner Wald and clambered up the slopes on foot, leaving the jeep to meet us at the top. At the summit restaurant the Russian military had made themselves very much at home; their jackets were off, their sleeves rolled up; they had brought picnic baskets and were swilling beer; several soldiers were playing concertinas. They were all enjoying the warmth and sunshine.

Our officers were very much on their dignity, their uniforms neat

The British Headquarters, Schönbrunn Palace, in 1945.

Graves of Russian and Austrian soldiers killed in the battle for Vienna.

White Among the Reds

and correct. They glanced contemptuously at the Russians. Our Colonel ushered us up to a table. As we approached the Russians began whispering among themselves, obviously about us. One man was heard to say: 'Hush! They might be interpreters!' We ordered drinks and exchanged remarks quietly and decorously.

There was one Russian officer, stocky, broad-shouldered, with a strong oriental slant to his widely-spaced eyes – a mischievous face. He kept glancing our way. His cap was perched on the back of his head. He was much the worse for drink. He kept suggesting toasts, shouting, and slapping his neighbours on the back, spilling their drink. Yet none of them protested. He then burst into song and came staggering across in our direction. His companions were laughing but with embarrassment. We had paid no attention, but now that the drunk was lurching towards us, our Colonel rose demonstratively and led us away to his jeep. The Russian did not follow and the episode was soon forgotten, though his striking face remained in my memory.

We picnicked in the woods and rested under the pines. The Colonel started telling me a lengthy story about frogs. I dozed off and dreamt of hordes of frogs frolicking all over me. We returned sun-tanned, pleasantly tired and hungry to an evening of food and song. De Becque joined us with a French girl and Kovalev with a Russian girl. Some of our interpreters had very pleasing voices.

Such excursions were rare. We lacked transport. Instead we went to the local cinema, or lounged in each other's rooms, or walked in the park.

When we went to see *Ivan der Schreklicke*, the crowds there looked sick and miserable. All round, people were coughing and sneezing. But young girls giggled and children kept running about. People shoo-ed at them, contributing to the noise. Just in front of us, a man had a fit. Many of the men in the audience were without a leg, or an eye, but they were few, as most of the Viennese menfolk were still prisoners of war, or had been carted off by the Russians as labour. Soviet soldiers arriving late, in order not to inconvenience the audience, bent down, their straight backs making a complete right angle and advanced thus to their seats. It was fascinating to watch a whole line of them making their way in this manner. We were repeatedly sprayed with disinfectant. Once I got it straight in the face.

Everything Suspended

Though we mixed with the local population, officially we were not allowed to fraternise. This applied particularly to the Austrian prisoners of war working on the repairs of the Schönbrunn Palace. But when our officers went by, many of the prisoners saluted. They would bow and smile at us, especially after I had offered them cigarettes.

In the park occasionally we would meet groups of Russian officers whom we had got to know. We would stop and chat, to the astonishment of the Austrians, who did not expect to see the British and the Russians enjoying each other's company.

One evening Alec, my friend from the Intelligence Corps, and I came across a grave with a wooden cross, on which were inscribed the words 'Here lies a Russian without documents.' The words were badly mis-spelt. The grave was smothered in weeds. We decided to clean it up. An Austrian gardener watched us and later we saw him cleaning up other graves and planting shrubs on them. It was sad to see so many graves.

General Winterton had his own adventure with a Russian grave. There was one under his office window at the Schönbrunn Palace, right in the middle of the lawn. Russians often buried their dead wherever they found them. Winterton ordered its removal. This was done, but the next morning, there it was back again in its original position. Annoyed, he insisted that it be taken away. The same thing again; the grave was back in its original place. So he ordered the reburial to be done officially with military honours. A Guard of Honour was produced and the grave was ceremoniously moved to a suitable corner of the lawn, with a wreath placed upon it. There it remained in peace.

Now that more of the Commission were in Vienna and the number of women had risen to three, we were moved from the Park Hotel into new quarters in the Viktoria Hotel. Here at last we were supplied with hot water and were able to have a bath. Several male interpreters were billeted with us for our protection and a sentry was allotted to us till it had been made clear that these premises were occupied by British personnel and people stopped breaking into them. The men billeted with us protested at having to move there. Most of them had already found themselves comfortable quarters elsewhere. They were

The Mayor of Vienna speaking.

Allied Generals.

Red Army troops marching past.

Red Army troops marching past.

Red Army troops marching past.

British troops, unarmed, marching past.

civilians; army officers seemed to take things more easily in their stride.

Mr Williams, the British Consul, was still living in the Park Hotel. He became our focal point. He was unaffected by the strange surroundings. He sat quietly of an evening at his table, reading his *Times* and doing the crossword, as relaxed as though he were in his own surroundings at home. The first time Janet and I joined him, he put down his paper reluctantly. Tentatively I started telling him of my mixed feelings about the Russians; Alec, to whom I could speak freely, was so often away on official trips. Mr Williams responded immediately. Though he neither spoke Russian nor came into direct contact with the Russians, yet he seemed to understand and sympathise with my feelings. He did not say much, but it was a comfort to be able to share my doubts. However, invariably as soon as I started talking, I would be called away to deal with some problem requiring an interpreter.

One evening Janet and I picked up an Australian rugby-player in the hotel bar. He was on his way to the UK and was excited at the prospect of seeing the old country for the first time. His accent sent our officers scattering. Mr Williams arrived, took in the situation and invited both us and the rugby-player to dine with him at his table. He produced his own wines, and we celebrated and gave the Australian a generous send-off.

On August 19th a number of us were invited to attend the unveiling of the newly-erected Russian War Memorial, which both among the Allies and the Viennese was commonly referred to as the 'Memorial to the Unknown Looter'. It had become the subject of constant mirth – a gift to local wits.

The day was sunny and warm. I was invited with our senior officers into the Allied VIP enclosure at the foot of the Monument. The small detachment of our troops was only allowed to attend as 'spectators' and were therefore without rifles. Had they attended as 'participants', the Russians might have claimed that we had officially entered Vienna and should therefore carry responsibility for feeding the population.

Everything Suspended

In their summer khaki shorts our soldiers looked almost boyish, with trim, neat figures.

The Monument itself was shrouded. Red Army soldiers encircled it, while a host of pot-bellied, straight-backed generals strutted around barking out orders. The Commanding Officer inspected the troops. In response to his greeting, they shouted back in unison: 'We wish you health, Comrade General!' The generals mounted a platform. Among them we spotted those we knew – Morozov, the Chief of Staff and Blagodatov, the Commandant. Below stood the Russian officials, officers and soldiers not on parade, and the Viennese populace.

It was a solemn moment. To the strains of the Soviet National Anthem, the Monument was unveiled with a terrifying 'swish' of rockets, which burst in a fountain of colour above our heads, and came crashing down on top of us, some still in flames. Guns fired simultaneously. Instead of standing to attention, we ducked to avoid the rockets; the crowd was hurriedly pushed back into safety. As the anthem resounded a second time, fountains came into play reflecting the sunlight merrily.

Then came the speeches. Colonel-General Gusev, the victor of Vienna, a portly figure in a light green uniform, was the main speaker. Renner, the President pro-tem of the Austrian Republic followed. (Our diplomats kept away from the ceremony owing to his presence. He had been proclaimed President by the Russians and we did not wish to recognise their right to appoint anyone). Then came Körner, the city mayor, apparently a great hero; he was greeted by the Austrians with tremendous applause. After the speeches the generals lined up and advanced solemnly to place wreaths at the foot of the Monument.

The march past followed. Our Brigadier Palmer, Colonel Samych of America and General Du Peyrat of France, took the salute with the Russian generals. The Red Army came first. They looked very tough; their uniforms were clean, but faded, some torn in places; some of their boots were held together by string. They were small men. They stared intently forward; one could well believe that they would always forge ahead, regardless of obstacles and that they would be capable of standing up to immense strain. Their faces were expres-

White Among the Reds

sionless. Our men following them looked pink and white by comparison, but much larger. The Americans, long and lanky, slouched past. Bringing up the rear came small groups of even shabbier Soviet soldiers. They were preceeded by banners and were headed by Major-Generals.

By now some of our officers were getting bored. They began exchanging critical remarks about the Russians' uniform and their unkempt appearance. As these last small contingents passed, the officers sniggered at such a sorry sight of the so-called 'mighty Red Army'. I happened to turn round. There, just behind us, stood Major Kovalev, the Russian liaison officer. He could not have understood the words spoken, but the general tone of the remarks would be obvious, even to a foreigner. I smiled at him. There was an awkward silence.

He said: 'Those men are all that are left of the divisions that captured the city,' and walked away. I felt ashamed and passed his remark on to our officers. They pulled themselves together and remained silent for the rest of the time. Up on the platform I was grateful to see our Brigadier Palmer still correctly at the salute.

When the troops had passed, civilians followed – pathetic groups of local communists and handicapped individuals. They limped and staggered past, many on crutches. They held up their fists and Brigadier Palmer also 'took the fist'. One of the slogans carried past was 'Glory to the Red Army who saved Vienna from the Atom Bomb.' We tried to puzzle that one out!

Going back to the hotel, I thought over the morning's events and of what the Memorial meant to the Russians. Their casualties had been enormous. Obviously they still felt the horror of it all. But how was it that, with the war hardly over, we had already drifted so far apart? That we had not shared in their feelings, and that we, their war-time allies, had in fact mocked their dead?

5

Meeting of the Commanders-in-Chief

Anxiously we waited. Marshal Koniev was suffering from an ulcer or was this merely an excuse to avoid calling a meeting of the C-in-Cs? The future of the Allied Commission and relations between the Allies depended on their getting together quickly before the strains between East and West became uncontrollable. And would these four men be the kind to heal the breach? Would they care? What were they like? These questions plagued us as the huge administrative machine of the ACA marked time.

At last an invitation arrived from Marshal Koniev to attend the inaugural Allied Council meeting at the Imperial Hotel, the Russian HQ, on the following day.

I hurried down to the Imperial Hotel with one of our Russian-speaking officers to deliver McCreery's acceptance. We had forgotten the pass which was now required for Soviet establishments and marched straight in, my companion shouting: 'You want a pass? What nonsense!' and the Russian guards let us through.

That whole night Alec and I spent translating into English the Soviet draft Press Communiqué and draft Proclamation to the Austrian people.

We started working in the Park Hotel; then, as so often happened, the electric light failed. The only electric generator was in the Schönbrunn Palace. It was past midnight and we had no transport; we were forced to commandeer a car. Embarrassed, we stood in the

White Among the Reds

middle of the street and stopped the first vehicle. It was driven by an elderly lady, an Austrian Countess. She was amused and willingly drove us to the Palace. There we continued working till four in the morning, lost in the silence of this immense place, and fed with cups of coffee and sandwiches by the soldiers on duty.

That same morning, August 23rd, the first Allied Council meeting took place and was followed by a review of the Allied Forces in the Schwarzenberg Platz. Now we would see the C-in-Cs.

Issued with special passes, we British stood in a small group beside the Allied Press at a corner of the huge, empty square. There were no Austrians present; the square was barred off and Russian soldiers lined the pavement. They looked very young, with broad, Slav features and well-scrubbed necks and ears. Colonel Kapustin, a big man with heavy black eyebrows and a square black beard, was in command. Occasionally he spat and ground his spit into the earth with the toe of his shiny black boot. An American woman journalist broke through the guards and ran across the square.

Colonel Kapustin turned on a soldier: 'Why did you let her through?'

The soldier retorted: 'I didn't; she forced her way through.'

I chatted with the Soviet soldiers in front of us till I happened to mention: 'Here come our men,' as the British contingent took up their positions; the soldiers then fell silent.

The Allied troops were in position in front of the tribune; to the side, the four Allied bands were drawn up, the Moroccan goat mascot motionless beside the Moroccan band. Excited, we waited in silence. This was the moment we had been expecting so long.

With a flick of the Russian conductor's baton, and a roll of drums, the four bands playing together struck up the National Anthems. The Commanders-in-Chief had appeared. They stood saluting on the dais, the Allied flags unfurled above their heads. We strained to get a better view, I especially of McCreery; on him depended our relations with the Russians.

Lieutenant-General Sir Richard McCreery was a tall, lean cavalry officer, his long face reserved, austere. The American General Mark Clark was as tall as McCreery. His forage cap exposed more of a long, arrogant face and long nose; there was something of the Red Indian

Meeting of the Commanders-in-Chief

about him. Marshal Koniev was a broad-shouldered figure with a rounded face and high Slav cheek-bones, and General Bethouart, a distinguished-looking Frenchman with small clear-cut features. All four so very different.

Marching abreast the C-in-Cs inspected the troops. We watched them intently studying their faces and movements, seeking a clue to their personality. General Mark Clark swung gracefully along beside General McCreery's stiff march; McCreery had a gammy leg. The other generals remained on the dais, Alec in their midst as interpreter, one hand as usual resting on his hip, and grinning down at us.

The march past followed – Russians, British, Americans and French. The Russians paraded in steel helmets, marching in close formation with bayonets fixed and goose-stepping – a horrible sight; it made them look like robots. The tips of their bayonets were perilously near the ears of the men in front; some of these were bloodstained. Our men were still in shorts. But the Russians had been impressed by their actual entry into Vienna, according to Major Kovalev, the liaison officer. He told us how a group of Russians had 'commandeered' a stock of wine and concealed it under the straw of their cart; they then stopped outside an inn for a drink. As they were entering, they spotted the first British jeep appearing, its flag flying, in the distance. They watched its approach and then went inside. There, they could hear the British vehicles rolling past. When they came out they felt under the straw to make sure their bottles were safe. Not a single one remained!

The revue had been a demonstration of Allied military unity, at least on the surface. Throughout, the C-in-Cs had faced forward. There had been no exchange of words or glances. Nevertheless the four armies were now officially in Vienna, the Allied Council had met and with relief the ACA settled down to its job.

6

We Were Dismayed

Russian drunkenness, looting, rape – the British in the ACA indulged in orgies of condemnation. They rivalled the Press at home in producing horrific stories stemming mostly from the Austrians. Our Interpreters' Pool talked of nothing else, gloating over them. All the interpreters and translators had now arrived. They had been waiting in Rome where the most hair-raising stories of Russian behaviour were circulating.

We of the Advance Party had been as credulous and as sanctimonious when we arrived, but now we were dismayed. We had seen our own soldiers collapse drunkenly onto the ground.

As for looting, when a Nazi was arrested all four Allies raced to his home to carry off everything moveable before the Austrian police arrived. (The police were supposed to take custody, but by the time they were on the premises nothing remained). Our officers furnished their Messes and offices with looted ('liberated' it was euphemistically called) furniture. A friend of mine in London boasted of the number of chandeliers he had 'liberated' and brought home with him to the UK. I was tempted myself.

But we Westerners looted discreetly. The Russian soldiers displayed their loot openly. Everything hung from their belts – household goods, toys, and I even saw one man with a car tyre hanging from his belt. Watches many Russians were seeing for the first and probably last time; the temptation was too great.

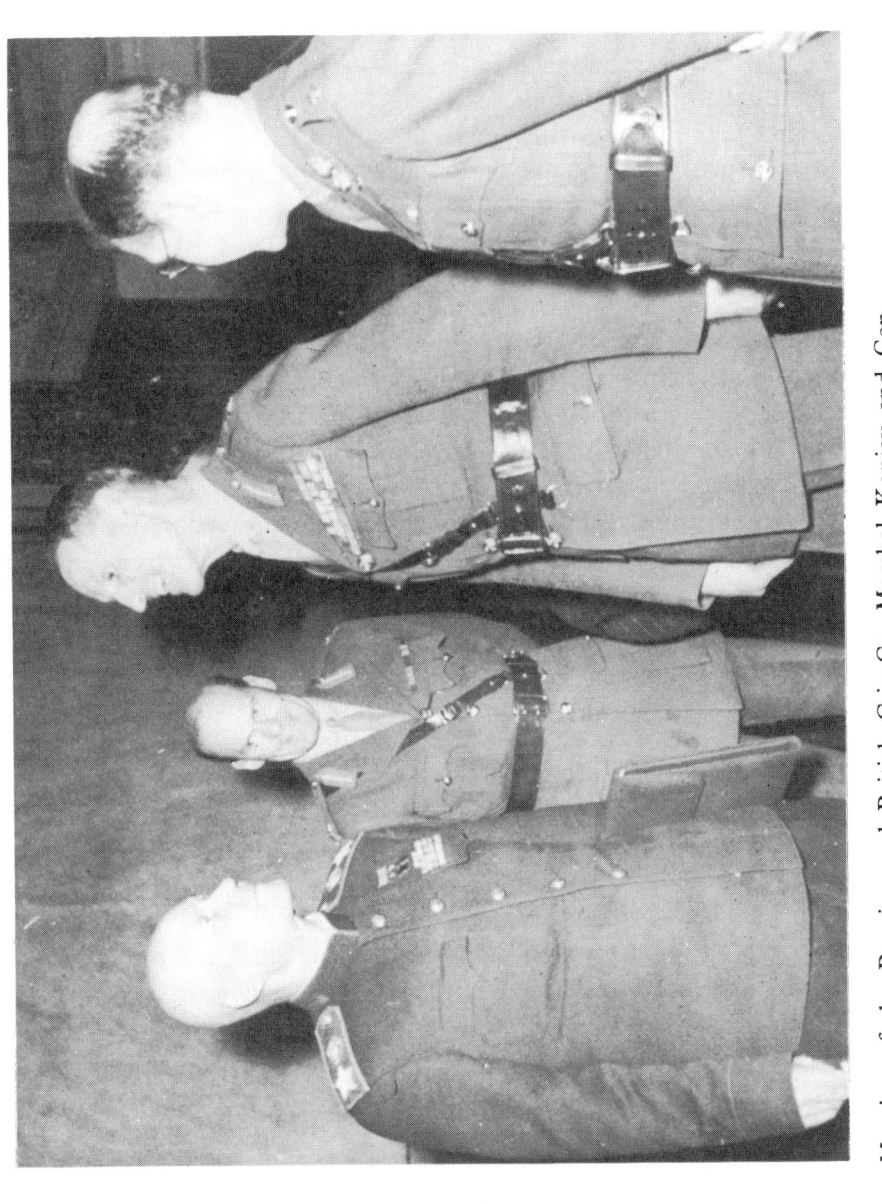

Meeting of the Russian and British C-in-Cs, Marshal Koniev and Gen. McCreery with Gen. Packard (centre) and interpreter (right).

White Among the Reds

As regards rape the Russians were guilty, but then local girls strolled in the parks at night with Soviet soldiers, and in the streets Austrian girls wore make-up which to the Soviet soldiers meant prostitutes.

That people should be shocked at times by the crudeness of the Soviet army was understandable, but with this wholesale public condemnation by the British as a body, how could we be expected to act in a natural and friendly manner with people we condemned as monsters? What was official policy towards the Russians? Were we or were we not supposed to treat them as Allies?

I appealed to Colonel Pryce-Jones, an Intelligence officer on the staff of General Winterton, our Deputy C-in-C. He assured me that official policy remained the same, to establish good relations with the Russians and to make a success of our work with them here in Vienna. He explained the general attitude by the fact that our generals did not care much one way or the other and were swayed by the nearest influence, often Austrian. Others followed their lead. But a report had been sent to London by an Intelligence officer pointing out that from the attitude taken up by our people here, one would think that the Austrians and not the Russians had been our Allies during the war.

This was reassuring. But such is the influence of generally held views and attitudes – and all those around us were permeated with fear of the Russians – that we ourselves were affected and were led into the most ridiculous situations.

On a particularly black night as we hurried home through the dark streets we heard shouts. Afraid of meeting drunken Russian soldiers we tried to slip past unnoticed keeping to the other side of the street. A man had fallen into a hole in the road and whenever he called for help passers-by rushed away. We had the sense to turn back and see what was the matter. We pulled him out. Then a British soldier appeared, took fright as he could not make out, in the dark, who we were, changed direction and headed straight for the hole. We shouted which only made him start running. We had to grab him to stop him falling in!

Colonel Miasnikov, Soviet Deputy of the Internal Affairs Division,

We Were Dismayed

once told me: 'The Austrians spend their time spreading rumours. They gossip to you about us, but they also gossip to us about you!'

Russians were afraid of us too. Our troops marched daily in the park, rehearsing for a parade. A Russian soldier who happened to be there was so frightened of being caught watching the British that he scrambled up the nearest tree, hid among the branches and then managed to fall out right into the midst of the marching troops. He broke his leg and it was some time before he was helped, as Standing Orders did not cover such an eventuality.

By chance we met a British journalist in the park. I immediately inveigled him into the hotel for tea. I had invited a few friends. We attacked him; we pointed out that the British Press when writing about the Russians concentrated solely on horror stories. Why?

He replied: 'We hear nothing else about them.'

'Do any of you speak Russian?' I asked. 'Have you met any Russians?' His answer was: 'No.' 'Then where do you get your material?'

'From Austrian friends mostly and some from the British in the ACA.'

I asked him whether he had personally ever seen any such horrors. No, he had not.

'Nor have I,' I told him although my job entailed mixing with them most of the time. There were beastly incidents but not on the scale the Press maintained. I went on to describe our contacts with the Russians and I told him what we had learnt about them.

'Well, this is all an eye-opener!' he exclaimed.

As I talked I criticised the Austrians for exaggerating stories and inciting the Western Allies against the Russians, forgetting that we had an Austrian guest among us. But she nodded in assent and said the Russians were uncouth, but not the brutes they were made out to be. She told us how the night before at the Opera two Soviet soldiers had forced their way into her box, pushed themselves to the front, so that she and the friend with her, sitting behind them, could see very little. The soldiers looked round the auditorium, started whispering, then with red faces removed their caps. Next, looking very embarrassed they got up, pushed the ladies to the front, and sighing sat down in the back seats. Then they burst out laughing and rushed out.

She spoke of the great generosity of the ordinary Red Army man. 'If he has anything you need, he will give it to you willingly,' she told us. 'He loots but he gives away as easily.' I remembered the soldiers emptying their pockets for the Vlassov prisoners. Then she added: 'And we were their enemies.' Remarkable and impressive statements from an Austrian. We were glad the journalist heard them.

By permitting the Austrians to complain to us about the Soviets and by taking their stories seriously, we encouraged them to forget they had fought against us. They became too friendly, clutching at opportunities to curse Hitler and the Nazis. We released a flood of complaints not only about the Russians but about conditions generally. Alec threatened to make a record and to play it as soon as any Austrian addressed him.

And they cadged. If an Austrian approached, we braced ourselves for the inevitable request. In the streets we were constantly stopped by Austrians begging for a bit of bread. We gave them our cigarettes. When we tried to explain why we were unable to give them food, they did not believe us; they did not believe there was rationing in the UK; they thought they were the only people who were having to go short. No doubt the Viennese were underfed, but now that with the entry of our troops we had finally agreed to take part in the provision of food, they took it for granted and demanded more. Many of the local British were hungry, but they did not complain.

It was at least understandable when the Austrians begged for food, but they took it for granted that we would be willing to go out of our way to oblige them. Total strangers pestered us for such things as theatre and cinema tickets when these were sold out (the military were always allowed free entry).

Alec with his kind manner was besieged by requests. One gentleman who approached him had a circus of three lions and two tigers. They were hungry and he wondered whether he might bring them to the Intelligence Mess to eat up the remains of the meals. Alec imagined the face of his Brigadier who had little sense of humour at the sight of the lions and tigers at the Mess table. With difficulty he replied seriously that he was sorry but it was out of the question.

Everything we did for the Austrians was taken for granted by them. Nor were they keen to work, even when it meant rebuilding their

We Were Dismayed

own city; it was doubtful whether they would achieve much in the next month's efforts of communal labour to clear the rubble from Vienna. We suspected that they only put themselves down for work because they hoped to get a meal; if it really looked like hard work, they packed up and went home.

Very quickly they learnt what was obtainable from our NAAFI, and refused money. I gave up going to the hairdresser because only cigarettes were accepted in payment. We were not allowed to give them away and we lost the right of duty-free cigarettes because so many were being used as currency. I tried to get my watch mended but in payment I was expected to give a bottle of gin. For mending our radio they demanded a bottle of cordial.

We resented this strongly, particularly so as Austria had hardly suffered at all during the war; her troubles only started at the very end when the Russians overran the country.

It was only in the Austrian Ministry of the Interior that our criticism was tempered. The Ministers were mostly from pre-Hitler days; all had suffered under the Nazis. One Bergen-Wallenegg had been in Buchenwald; he was a mere skeleton with nervous, twitching fingers. We waited for the meeting in a dark, unheated, damp room. An American officer with us sitting there, fat and prosperous-looking, his buttocks overlapping the chair, seemed out of place. During the meeting the Austrian Ministers were subdued and kept to business; their manner was reserved and dignified. There was no mention of Buchenwald. My criticism was silenced.

7

The ACA gets down to Work

The Allied Commission for Austria settled down to govern the country. Its Divisions and sub-committees were set up and interpreters were allotted to each. I was attached to the Internal Affairs Division. If I was free, I was sent to other meetings.

These took on a more formal aspect. We interpreters sat tense beside our delegates often watching others grope helplessly for the correct words. Interpreters had their own idiosyncrasies. One Frenchman was always 'uncovering beauty' instead of 'booty', another interpreter hurried into spoonerisms and talked of 'hole shells' and 'build bridging'. Charlie Thayer interpreting for General Gruenther, the American Deputy C-in-C, used the Yugoslav word for troops 'trupy' which in Russian means corpses. Solemnly he announced that American corpses would march in from the north, British corpses from the south and French corpses from the west!

The Russian general's comment was: 'We'll certainly have some cemetery here!' Charlie was also heard to say 'niet' on a rare occasion when General Gruenther had expressed his agreement to a Soviet proposal.

The general protested: 'Charlie, I know perfectly well that "niet" does not mean "yes"!' There was disagreement on policy between the State Department to which Charlie belonged and the American military. The Russian general waited, keenly interested, for the American delegation to agree amongst themselves.

The ACA gets down to Work

Delegates when they became excited forgot the interpreter and raced ahead, the interpreter trying at one and the same time to interrupt the delegate and to keep pace with the translation. Once when the translation came out all wrong, to my embarrassment I heard myself let out a slightly hysterical laugh.

The Russian delegate at my side enquired: 'Just how old are you?'

When stumped for a translation we had to invent ways of extracting the meaning. With medical terms the delegate could be asked to use Latin; with parts of an aircraft he could be asked to draw the part. Only once was I completely baffled. At a financial meeting the delegates had reached an impasse.

Speaking ponderously, the Russian addressed the British delegate: 'Well, you and I under the table.' I asked him what he meant.

'It's quite clear', he replied. 'I said: "You and I under the table" '. I explained that I did not understand what he meant. Surely he was not suggesting they should actually climb under this table?

'No, of course not!' He was impatient.

'Then could you please use another expression?'

'It is clear enough,' he said. We got no further.

The Russian word for 'pit-props' was a word I could never remember; it cropped up constantly. I had to write it down before each meeting on the cuff of my shirt sleeve.

The ACA Divisions had to decide first on procedure. How should outstanding problems be tackled? Each of the four Allies had firm ideas and they all differed. Meetings dragged on.

In the Internal Affairs Division, Brigadier Verney chaired the meetings. He arrived with his proposals ready. He listened attentively to the others, jotting down an occasional note, and allowed sufficient time for each delegate to feel he had been able to express his point of view fully. The Frenchman wove his points intricately and elaborately into a stylised whole; the American brought up subjects that had no apparent connection with procedure; the Russian hesitated about saying anything definite. When Verney decided that all had held forth sufficiently he put down his pencil, broke into the speeches, put forward his prepared proposals, referred to them as a 'compromise of the suggestions you have made here to-day,' and without pausing thanked the delegates for 'having agreed to them unanimously.'

At one meeting the speech-making took up a couple of hours, the decision, five minutes. 'Denazification,' 'Extension of the Influence of the Austrian Administrative Machine,' 'Frontier Control' and 'Posts, Telegraphs and Telephones,' all these were despatched to sub-committees of experts, who were to look into them and report back to the Committee in ten days' time. The Committee was to reassemble in each case forty-eight hours after receiving their report.

Brigadier Verney was replaced by Mr Nott-Bower, our ACA Chief of Police, a tall, willowy man with a red face and grey hair drawn back off a high forehead. He had a quiet, aloof manner. The silver on his black uniform was imposing. He worked along the same lines as Verney. I could see him doing *The Times* crossword during the speech-making period. The Russians were impressed by our methods. They ceased making speeches, and Colonel Ilichev, wasting no more time or words, nodded his agreement with our proposals. Sometimes he opposed with us the French and Americans who wanted more discussion.

When the Committee passed to matters of principle the real difficulties started. There was total lack of understanding between the Western powers and the Russians. At every meeting Colonel Ilichev repeated: 'I disagree' or 'Niet', the famous Russian 'No' that resounded throughout the Western world. It became the symbol of Russian obstruction. Ilichev's pale face was expressionless. The other delegates shifted in their chairs, but no amount of persuasion made Ilichev change his mind; nor did he give any explanation.

At a meeting on 'Freedom of Movement', he insisted that only certain categories of workers should be issued with special passes allowing them to move freely about the country. The rest of the population was excluded from free movement as well as the Allied personnel without special passes. Mr Nott-Bower was in despair. Why stop anyone from moving about freely? What we did not know at the time was that Soviet citizens were not allowed to move around freely in their own country.

In a Public Security discussion, Col. Ilichev refused to agree to the setting up of a permanent Police Mission to supervise and assist the Austrian police, thus taking minor matters out of the hands of the

The ACA gets down to Work

Internal Affairs Division. He insisted that the Internal Affairs Division should deal with every problem as it arose.

Over lunch and a bottle of wine, Mr Nott-Bower and I discussed the situation. He was despondent. He told me it was useless for him to remain in Vienna (he was Deputy Commissioner of the Metropolitan Police). He had come to set up a responsible, politically-independent police force with the necessary sophisticated equipment. Instead he was expected to deal with the supply of boots, transport and so on.

I tried to explain that this was the Russians' first contact with Western ideas. Their Communist Party controlled all aspects of life in their country; they could not understand how such a sensitive instrument of power as a police force could be 'politically independent'. They must be allowed time to learn more of Western ways. As for giving sophisticated equipment to the Austrian police the Russians would never agree to supply the Austrians with equipment their own people lacked.

With the bottle emptied we felt more optimistic and I persuaded Mr Nott-Bower to try and meet his Russian colleagues socially so that both sides could get to know each other better. He promised to think over what I had said.

All four Allies were in agreement on one occasion. The Legal Division was called in to advise on a legal point. The four lawyers were asked to give their opinion. They began, each one pleading his cause with eloquence, dramatic gesture and at great length and each one expressing a totally different opinion. Miasnikov tried to stop his lawyer by pulling at his coat and whispering: 'Cut it short!' but without success. We sat mesmerised. Finally the chairman intervened, thanked the lawyers and begged them to withdraw. The meeting was left confused and exhausted, but it was agreed unanimously never again to consult the lawyers!

Colonel Ilichev and Lieut-Col. Miasnikov were polite to Mr Nott-Bower. They admired him but at first were not at ease in his presence. They chatted to me before a meeting; as soon as he entered, they withdrew.

But some time later when a group of us were having a drink with the two Russians whom we had met in the Park Hotel dance hall, Mr

Nott-Bower appeared, edging along the hall, in what he must have thought an inconspicuous manner. He was clasping his jacket over something protruding underneath. Ilichev asked me to call him over. Mr Nott-Bower hesitated, then came across. Ilichev pointed to his jacket. With a grin, Mr Nott-Bower brought out a bottle of whisky. Both Russians jumped up; beaming they clapped him on the back and insisted on offering drinks all round. They had discovered he was human.

Russian generals were unpredictable. The first conference between the British and Russian Air Force Chiefs never got off the ground. Our Air Commodore refused to attend; he did not wish 'to have anything to do with these Russians.' He was replaced by his second-in-command, Group Captain Michael Dawnay, a big man with a cheerful, friendly manner. He and I together with the International Secretariat staff waited for the Russian Air Chief, Major-General Miachkine. In marched a broad-shouldered officer, with an oriental slant to widely-spaced eyes and a smile hovering over a round face. He seemed so very familiar to me – yes – the drunkard at the café on the top of the Kahlenberg! He glanced around and spotted me.

He burst out laughing and exclaimed as he came to greet me: 'We are old friends!' Now that I saw what a cheerful, care-free individual he was, I realised that on the Kahlenberg we British must have appeared too pompous for him to be able to resist his little joke.

As we stood smiling at each other, Michael began convening the meeting. Miachkine interrupted him. With a sweeping gesture that embraced the Secretariat, he said:

'All this can wait; there's lots of time.' He sat down and leaning confidentially across towards Michael, he announced: 'I want to know all about football.' We were taken aback, but he went on: 'I want to know how it is played in England. I want to understand the difference between how you play and how we play.' Michael, a keen footballer himself, obliged. The two of them launched into a lengthy discussion of the game. The Secretariat sat waiting, their note-books open.

The clock struck one. Michael started. As Chairman he proposed closing the meeting and adjourning to lunch so that the conversation could be continued. Miachkine was delighted, adding that he would have to bring along with him his second-in-command, Lieut-Col. Zinoviev.

The four of us transferred to the Park Hotel bar. Over the drinks Michael and Miachkine, the Irishman and the Soviet-Mongolian, were off to a heated argument roaming mentally around the world, now serious, now bursting with merriment, at one moment glaring at each other aggressively, and the next clasping hands and calling each other 'my friend'. Michael wanted to know what Miachkine thought of the Germans and their fighting capacity.

'The German army was first class, the generals too,' Miachkine said. 'Political blunder lost them the war, the fools. They gave free rein to the Gestapo and the SS troops in the occupied territories. They roused the local populations against themselves. They drove them to unimaginable heights of patriotism and valour. Politics lost them the battles the army had won. Fortunately for us!' and Miachkine laughed. He was never far from laughter. They turned to considering the atom bomb.

'We'll annihilate each other if we all have the bomb; if we don't, the country that has it will conquer the world.' He did not appear to be worried about it.

They got on to material possessions and agreed, as Michael put it: 'material possessions tend to destroy the spirit of a people. It's the middle classes who are always aspiring to greater and greater wealth.' Miachkine nodded in sympathy. Michael continued: 'The bourgeoisie – they are solely interested in material comfort – they should be exterminated.'

'In the Soviet Union, we have done just that!' cried Miachkine. I protested; I was not going to translate such cynical remarks. They laughed at me.

As we rose to go into lunch, the General took me aside. Was I really upset by their conversation, he asked? I said I was. He assured me most earnestly, and for once he looked serious, that in spite of what he had said, he had never shot anyone, except in time of war; Michael and he understood each other well; they could allow themselves such exaggeration.

Over the meal, they surveyed the strategy of European wars. Both were impatient to say so much they out-shouted each other across the table; with gestures they tried to stem the other's flow of talk. They jabbed the air with knife and fork to emphasise their points. I could hardly keep up with them. My hands were waving too, as I implored them to speak one at a time. By the end I leant back exhausted. They were grinning and in spite of the talk they had managed to put away a substantial meal. Throughout Lieut-Col. Zinoviev had concentrated on his food without saying a word. If his job, as I suspected, was to keep a political eye on his superior it was a very difficult task. As we were leaving we realised the dining room was still – everyone was staring at us.

Going from meeting to meeting, I became a kind of Universal Aunt to the delegates, whispering to them what to do and explaining the behaviour of others. Some of the Russians were uncouth; they had never mixed in foreign circles. They were grateful for any hints on behaviour. For their part they were tolerant of our mistakes as regards their rank or Service; no doubt we must have made many faux pas of which we remained ignorant. At a meeting between a British Intelligence officer and a Russian I arrived late to find them standing at opposite ends of the empty room, gazing intently out of the windows. They had no idea how to deal with each other, without an interpreter. At a medical meeting, when I was also late, the Russian rushed out of his corner, exclaiming: 'At last I can come out into God's light!'

I found these Russian delegates easy to deal with. One Soviet Colonel told me I deserved the Order of the Red Star. I wondered how the people back home would view that!

Kiselev, the Soviet Political Adviser, was a different kind of delegate; he was a career diplomat. He had the Western diplomat's self-assurance. He was a polished and astute man. He looked and obviously felt quite at ease among foreigners; culturally he could hold his own among them. There was a reserve in him, which the military so obviously lacked. He was suave. The Political Advisers, the future Ambassadors, were meeting in the Imperial Hotel, the Russian HQ. They were discussing the future government of the country. I waited outside as the delegates all spoke English. I was asked to translate into Russian a document they had drawn up and to type it out in Russian and English. I explained that I was no typist, but I would do

The ACA gets down to Work

my best. I translated the document while the delegates sat around and chatted. There were no facilities for typing. Kiselev apologised, saying that it was the Russian lunch hour (5 p.m.) Everyone was out. He called the duty officer. The young man did not know where anything was kept. He gave me the keys to all the rooms and suggested I search around, which I did. I went through the empty HQ, unlocking rooms, opening drawers and cupboards. Security did not trouble Kiselev.

I found an English and Russian typewriter, paper and carbons and settled down. I could not find any dictionaries; I hoped for help with spelling from the duty officer, but he turned out to be Ukrainian and was unable to write Russian correctly.

Each delegate required a copy of the document in each language. When I had finished I distributed the English versions. The delegates looked at them puzzled. I had put the carbons in on the wrong side; the copies came out on the backs of the previous pages! I apologised and had to do them all over again. No one worried; the delegates had settled down to champagne and black caviar. They were arguing heatedly. Jack Nicholls, our delegate, maintained that the most difficult people to have dealings with were the Portuguese. Jack Earhardt, the American, exclaimed that the Portuguese were not nearly as bad as the Russians: they were quite impossible. Kiselev became thoughtful, then turning to me asked my opinion. I replied that I had not yet had a chance to judge. He made me promise to tell him later on.

Kiselev initialled my Russian texts with hardly a glance at them – a polite show of complete trust. He drew up a chair and settled me down with champagne and caviar singling me out for particular attention. He explained why my name was famous in Russia and told the delegates about my revolutionary great-grandfather. He was a young aristocrat, Ivan Poustchine, who played a leading role in a military uprising in St. Petersburg on December 14th, 1825. The conspirators became known as the Decembrists. They were demanding a Constitution and freedom for the serfs (Russia at that time was an absolute monarchy and the peasants were still serfs). My ancestor was sent to hard labour in Siberia for life. He was also famous for being the poet Pushkin's best friend. The Soviets revere the Decembrists as the first

Russian revolutionaries. In my family this ancestor was the black sheep.

The champagne went gradually to my head. I sat as though in state. When Kiselev had finished about my ancestor we rose and, escorted by him, I sailed out ahead of the delegates, feeling for the moment at least, very much a VIP.

A more difficult type of delegate to deal with was the 'party-trained' specialist, such as General Tsinev, Chairman of the Economic Division. He had complete self-assurance, but none of the diplomatic polish of a Kiselev. He spoke in accepted phraseology, never venturing an opinion or a turn of phrase of his own. When our delegate expressed regret that they had started working together at a time when subjects on which the two sides held completely different views were discussed, Tsinev replied amiably: 'But we are merely the instruments of our government. Naturally we oppose each other and will continue to do so. That has no influence on my good feelings towards you.' He was merely an instrument, never ruffled, roused or angry. He never acted spontaneously. He had a colourless personality.

Another 'party-trained' delegate was Akomova, a fat woman, untidy with high heels worn down at the sides, but with an intelligent, responsive face. She also spoke in accepted phraseology as though addressing a public meeting. Such delegates stood out from among the rank and file of the highly eccentric military.

I was asked to attend a meeting of the Executive Committee, the second highest organ of the ACA. Another officer was to begin the interpreting; I was to replace him later. I knew that our generals preferred male interpreters; also I had not been shown the agenda and had been unable to prepare for the meeting. I was very nervous.

We were in the American HQ and I waited in an ante-room. When I opened the door to go to the cloakroom, I found an American sentry outside. He called a Colonel in charge of security and together we three marched there and back. I thought that was carrying security a bit far!

The meeting had been going on for three hours when I was asked to take over. The three Western delegates were leaning heavily on

The ACA gets down to Work

the table. The Russian was sitting up straight. General Winterton eyed me gloomily as I took my place behind him. He remarked that he was so worn out, a woman had been provided for him, to which General Zheltov, the Soviet Deputy C-in-C and Political Commissar, replied cheerfully that in that case he would be willing to sit for many hours more. He looked relaxed and fresh. Russians never tire of talking.

I was so interested I forgot about myself and my nervousness. They were working at cross purposes. We, the French and the Americans relied on our experts and their sub-committees to work out acceptable proposals, which the senior generals would then decide how best to implement. The Russian experts were only allowed to put forward tentative suggestions. Their delegate on the Executive Committee, the Political Commissar, would then proceed to improve on them or discard them or make further suggestions. Thus what for us was agreed and final, was for the Russians a point of departure. Our decisions were made by the experts, theirs by their Political Commissar. As General Zheltov went on and on embroidering on subjects our generals considered closed, they became more and more frustrated. Winterton squirmed on his chair with impatience.

The American delegate shouted at Zheltov: 'One more suggestion from you, Alexis, and I shall start making further suggestions myself!'

'But surely we are here in the Executive Committee to make progress, to advance?' Zheltov seemed genuinely puzzled. 'Surely we are not here just to receive reports, and to stop there?'

It was disheartening to find such exasperation building up over mere differences of procedure.

At a previous meeting of the Executive Committee, Winterton, utterly exhausted, announced that for the last time he would put forward his proposals and he refused to talk further. He opened his brief and read it out, brushing aside the expert at his side, who tried to interrupt him. When he had finished, the Russian said: 'I agree!' Winterton had been reading out the Soviet proposals!

I was free after lunch one day and was walking towards our hotel, when a jeep suddenly braked beside me, a couple of our officers sprang out, bundled me into it and drove off at full speed. They rushed me to the American HQ explaining that a conference was in

White Among the Reds

progress between the C-in-Cs and there were no interpreters. A French interpreter had also been picked up. He and I were hurried into the conference room. I was dishevelled, my thoughts were in a whirl, but I had no time to be nervous. I concentrated so hard on what was being said that later I hardly remembered anything about the conference or how it went, but at least I had not bungled it. It was, I thought, an original way of being introduced to the Allied Council.

8

High-Level Entertainment

Should I or should I not accept an invitation to the Soviet October Revolution Anniversary party? This was the quandary I faced once more. I had no wish to celebrate a revolution, nor did I think it would be right for me to do so. But this anniversary had become the Soviet National Day. The invitation came from individuals whom I had grown to respect. I had received nothing but kindness and consideration from them. In spite of my anti-Soviet background, in all our dealings they had never caused me the slightest embarrassment. A refusal on my part would seem churlish. I wanted to go. I accepted.

I became involved, either as guest or interpreter, in a whole series of high level ACA entertainments. The Soviet October Revolution Anniversary party was the first. Owing to the difference in the Old and New Style Russian calendars, the October Revolution is celebrated on November 7th. Marshal Koniev, the Russian C-in-C, was to give a mammoth reception in the Hofburg Palace. Everyone of importance was invited. Major Kovalev, the Russian liaison officer, appeared in the Interpreters' Pool asking for a list of our senior British officers and officials in the ACA and visiting VIPs. The Secretariat drew up a list. When I handed it to Kovalev he glanced down it and with a smile and a nod, added my name at the bottom.

'You are getting an invitation too,' he said. Our officers were to interpret for the generals.

Brigadier Block, the new Chairman of the Internal Affairs Division,

White Among the Reds

a large man with plump features and a kindly disposition, realising that I would be on my own, suggested that I accompany him. I was grateful. The invitation was from 4 to 7 p.m. but we were all instructed to arrive at 4.15 before our C-in-C, General McCreery, made his entrance.

We edged up to the Palace in a convoy of official cars, the flags displaying the rank of each guest. At the entrance Colonel Ilichev and Lieut-Col. Miasnikov, Brigadier Block's Soviet counterparts, detached themselves from a group awaiting their guests, and with smiles and hand-shakes escorted us inside. Ahead stretched an imposing stairway, brilliantly floodlit. Ilichev directed us towards it. It was like stepping onto a stage. Cameras clicked and we could hear the whirring of film as we ascended, Brigadier Block taking refuge behind me. Completely blinded by the lights, we nearly bumped into General Morozov, the Chief of Staff, and three other generals standing at the top in full-dress light blue uniforms, their chests covered with rows of medals. Morozov greeted us and led us into the main hall where, beneath a palm tree and a huge candelabra, the focus of innumerable floodlights, stood Marshal Koniev, the multitude of his jewelled decorations shimmering in the brilliant light. General Zheltov, his Deputy, stood behind him. He introduced us. With cameras clicking and whirring more loudly than ever and the lights hot on our faces, we shook hands. There was a stillness, a feeling of utter repose about the Marshal, standing motionless, calm, seemingly oblivious of all the attention centred upon him. He smiled, looking straight into our faces. Then we slipped into the obscurity behind him and watched with the others, the photographers converging on General Mark Clark, the American C-in-C, to be followed shortly afterwards by General McCreery.

We were escorted to the buffet. It was a fine spread on a white damask cloth covering an immense table running the whole length of the wall. But all I got was a teaspoonful of caviar; the Austrians (the whole government was present) made short work of it all. I had never seen so much food go so quickly. We noticed the Russian generals, a whole crowd of them displaying magnificent decorations, stood back, waving the waiters towards the guests. They looked very pleased with themselves. They spoke of the anniversary as 'this festive

High-Level Entertainment

day' or 'our holiday'. An old Russian priest was there beside the table; I was in good company. He remained the centre of a group of young Russian officers for the rest of the evening. Everyone was in a festive and lively mood. I had to work hard as there were no interpreters among the general public.

We proceeded into the ballroom and listened to a fine Russian choir of a hundred voices, singing nostalgic, emotional national songs against what had become the normal barrage of floodlights and clicking cameras. The photographers ran wild among the audience. Some humorists maintained that the efforts of the photographers at a previous concert were not good enough for the NKVD (KGB) files; they had been told to do better this time.

In the interval we went out and drank vodka; then returned for more songs. In the second interval the generals had their dinner. We strolled off with our escorts and noticing a door opening and closing mysteriously I peered in. General Morozov and two American generals were leaning against a table laden with dozens of empty champagne bottles. Morozov kept shouting for more and opening bottle after bottle. He was swaying slightly. On seeing us, he waved us in and offered us champagne. We stood around drinking with them. Morozov kept seizing flowers out of the vases and thrusting them into my arms. Suddenly he asked me:

'What are you doing to-night?'

I said: 'Nothing special.'

'Do you play cards?' I nodded. 'Right then, I'll pick you up outside this place' and, turning to one of his numerous adjutants: 'Arrange the details', he ordered.

As the adjutant came over to me, I laughed, but another young man whispered: 'He means it. Please, do go away!' So we withdrew to the relief of our escorts, who were uncomfortable in the presence of the generals.

Brigadier Block was a solid, heavy individual, very upright and with an impressive appearance. A group of Russian generals rushed over to him. They were led by a tiny man, a Colonel-General Novikov, who had commanded the tanks at Stalingrad and then on to Vienna. He was treated with the greatest respect by the others. Novikov seized

Brigadier Block's red lapels and appeared to be trying to shake him. Still clinging on, he shouted up into the Brigadier's face:

'We beat the Germans together! Why should we now fight? In England and America there are bankers and capitalists who want war.' He took a firmer grip: 'But we mustn't fight each other. You must control these Wall Street warlords. We are sick and tired of war. We don't want to fight.'

Brigadier Block stood his ground, murmuring: 'What's it all about?' When I got a chance to translate he was amazed at the General echoing the Soviet Press with so much feeling. However, he listened patiently while Novikov seemed in his earnestness to be trying to climb up Block's massive front. Novikov demanded to know why England would not give India freedom and independence, and now that there was a Labour government, why did they continue the Conservatives' foreign policy? He pleaded over and over again: 'Why won't you try to understand us?'

The other generals, crowding round Block, repeated in a kind of Greek chorus: 'Yes, why won't you try to understand us?' and 'Why should we fight each other?' Block never got a chance to reply.

Novikov let go his grip on the Brigadier. He stood back and addressing the company in general declared solemnly: 'Russia now has two aims; firstly,' he struck his palm with the first finger of the other hand, 'to create the right conditions for her recovery and future well-being, and secondly,' he struck his palm with the first two fingers of the other hand, 'to ensure peace.' He shook hands warmly with Brigadier Block and the other British officers who had joined us. Then overcome with emotion he embraced them each in turn. They reacted superbly, giving no sign of astonishment or embarrassment.

During the rest of the evening General Novikov kept materialising at my side. When we finally parted he surprised me by saying:

'Give my love to your Mother, won't you. I would like to meet her.'

At about 8.15 most of the guests had left. The Brigadier and I were strolling around with Ilichev. We came across Miasnikov. He was very drunk, wandering unsteadily calling loudly for a girl: 'Lialia! Lialia! Where is she?' The others were laughing at him.

Ilichev led us into a room where the choir was dining at one very long table. Marshal Koniev had also entered. He was greeted in a traditional manner. The leading girl singer was lifted onto the table. She sang the words of a song of welcome as she presented the Marshal with a glass of wine. Rising to their feet, the whole choir – a hundred voices – took up the chorus. The Marshal emptied the glass in one go, as tradition prescribed. Again I was struck by his quiet, restrained manner. He made no unnecessary movement. The girl jumped down off the table and he kissed her on the forehead. He then settled down at the table with the choir. I was watching fascinated when I became aware of the Brigadier plucking at my sleeve. He looked extremely worried.

He whispered: 'I am the only non-Russian officer here. It's inconsiderate of us to stay on, isn't it? They may want to celebrate on their own.' He was right. I apologised.

As we walked out, escorted to the car by a crowd of lively Russian officers, they clasped my hand, and repeated over and over again: 'We all love you and we respect you very much, remember that always!' So much for Russian reticence, unapproachability and inscrutability, I thought. Englishmen in the same situation, would have taken leave of me as Brigadier Block did a moment later, with a: 'Thanks. 'Bye.'

Officers from Styria, Corinthia and Italy were pouring in for the races. It did not seem a very appropriate time for racing with the poverty all around us, but since the officers were there we were out to enjoy them. In their honour General McCreery gave a ball in the Schönbrunn Palace.

We girls rushed off to the hairdresser. There were so few curlers that as Janet's hair dried, they were taken out one by one and put into my hair. The hot water ran out and Olia's head was plunged into a basin of cold water. But we came out pleased with ourselves and hurried home to prepare the long evening dresses we had all managed to acquire. In my bath that evening by mistake I turned on the overhead shower and that was the end of my beautiful new hair-do!

The Palace looked magnificent, floodlighting illuminating its classical facade; the ballroom was lit by all the eight hundred lamps and candelabra, the antique furniture glistened with polish; a superb buffet was laid out and Viennese waltzes reverberated through the reception rooms, a setting fit for our girlish dreams.

Unfortunately our dreams were not realised. Our transport failed us. We waited a whole hour, while one of the officers searched for a car. When we finally arrived, our evening gowns were crumpled, our corsages wilting. In the ballroom the men all congregated round the bar; so many officers and all ignoring us sad wallflowers. We had become accustomed to the gallantry of the Americans, the French and the Russians and as we smiled fixedly we raged inside against these prosaic Englishmen. Even the Consul, Mr Williams, leant against the bar with the other men, and he was such a good dancer. . .

General McCreery being a teetotaller, there was little drink, a glass of wine per person, which infuriated the men. Some of the girls went home early. When it was all over, the men dispersed and we girls were left on our own once more without transport. Michael Dawnay, our Air Force cavalier, came to the rescue. He offered to take me home and then agreed to ferry the other ten girls home too. He was amused by our indignation, but it was heart-rending – such a glorious setting and such a dismal evening!

Mr Berthoud, Chairman of our Economic Division, gave a dinner for his colleagues and for the Allied Chiefs of Staff. I was to take care of General Morozov. This proved to be my special day.

The company was animated and friendly. Our catering had now reached a high standard. As we ate, General Morozov told me a little about himself. He was fond of reading and enjoyed driving out into the countryside, preferably with an attractive female companion. He described how driving through the Wiener Wald he had given a lift to a group of our ATS girls. On the way back, he had come across them again. They were carrying bunches of flowers, their sleeves were rolled up, their shirts unbuttoned at the top and they each had a flower in their hair. They were singing as they marched down. They made a charming picture. He picked them up. There was laughter and fun in the big car, till one of the girls asked him what he did. On hearing he was the Russian Chief of Staff, she gasped: 'A general?'

High-Level Entertainment

As he nodded, the girls pulled down their sleeves, buttoned up their shirts, pulled the flowers out of their hair and in spite of all his protestations, sat silent and demure all the way back to Vienna.

We talked of life and love. He assured me it was useless waiting for some 'fairy-tale prince' to marry; men were all more or less alike.

We were interrupted by the speeches. After the four Allied Heads of the Economic Division had spoken, I was called on to speak. I rose nervously to my feet and plunged in:

'We interpreters are doing our best to smooth things over for you, the delegates. We try to establish good relations. So after witnessing so much disagreement at meetings, it is particularly rewarding to see such friendly relations around this table' – and I sat down hurriedly.

General Morozov laughed at my nervousness. He admitted that he also hated speaking in public and was no good at it. He was constantly reproved, he said, for speaking out too openly. I was astonished since, as I told him, our people found they could get nothing out of him or out of any of the Russians. This surprised him; he maintained that it was the English who were reserved and never expressed their real thoughts or showed their real feelings.

Now General Morozov was called on to speak. He turned to me in a panic, begging me to help him and to say the right things for him. He would murmur something in my ear. I had been reading Churchill that afternoon. His words were still reverberating in my mind. As General Morozov and I rose to our feet and he began murmuring, I found the words flowing from me in a grandiose Churchillian richness with many a 'yea' and 'nay' (I never felt nervous when I was speaking for someone else). Our speech drew loud applause and caused Morozov to exclaim: 'It sounded Shakespearean!'

After this success, he grew braver and attempted to speak to the others in English; his good pronunciation impressed and delighted them. The dinner ended in the warmest atmosphere. As he was leaving, Morozov suddenly picked up my menu card and wrote: 'Miss Poustchine contributed most to the creation of friendly feelings between the Allied armies.' He signed it 'Lieut-General Morozov'. I gazed at the words with deep pleasure.

Only that morning, a Russian delegate had asked me to come into a private room where their documents were kept. Several Russian

White Among the Reds

officers were standing around, smiling broadly. The delegates made a little speech saying that for all the help I had given them, especially when they were starting out as delegates, I deserved the Order of the Red Star, and here was a token of their thanks. He handed me a Red Star Russian Army badge. I laughed and pinned it onto my blouse. Hastily he protested, saying that a Red Army badge should be treated with respect; it should only be worn on a correct uniform. I took it off and held it in my hand. Two such tributes made this my very special day.

Henry V, the film, was about to be shown in Vienna. General McCreery arranged for a gala opening performance, to be followed by his first reception of the Allies and the Austrian government in the Schönbrunn Palace. Lady McCreery flew in from the UK and I was asked to interpret for her.

It was a splendid occasion. Outside floodlighting threw great shadows of the guns and the mounted police over the front of the Palace. And this time the guests behaved in a manner befitting the setting. The Austrians bowed low and kissed Lady McCreery's hand. Some of the Russians, self-conscious and overwhelmed by the richness of the surroundings, rushed away before completing the reception line.

As soon as the guests were assembled, cocktails were served. Marshal Koniev was in a cheerful mood; he joked with Lady McCreery and she flirted graciously with him.

The buffet was opened for the general public. The generals were escorted into a special room where they had their own buffet, while a table was laid apart for the guests of honour: General Bethouart, the French C-in-C, General Mark Clark, Mr Mack, our Political Adviser, Chancellor Figl, the Austrian Prime Minister and Marshal Koniev. His ADC, Captain Beloussov, sat behind him and I was seated between Lady McCreery and Marshal Koniev.

Special dishes were prepared for the Marshal, because of the ulcer he was supposed to have. He was not pleased. He barely touched the soup or the ice-cream. He was out to have a good time among friends and in a relaxed atmosphere. He kept trying to offer toasts. He

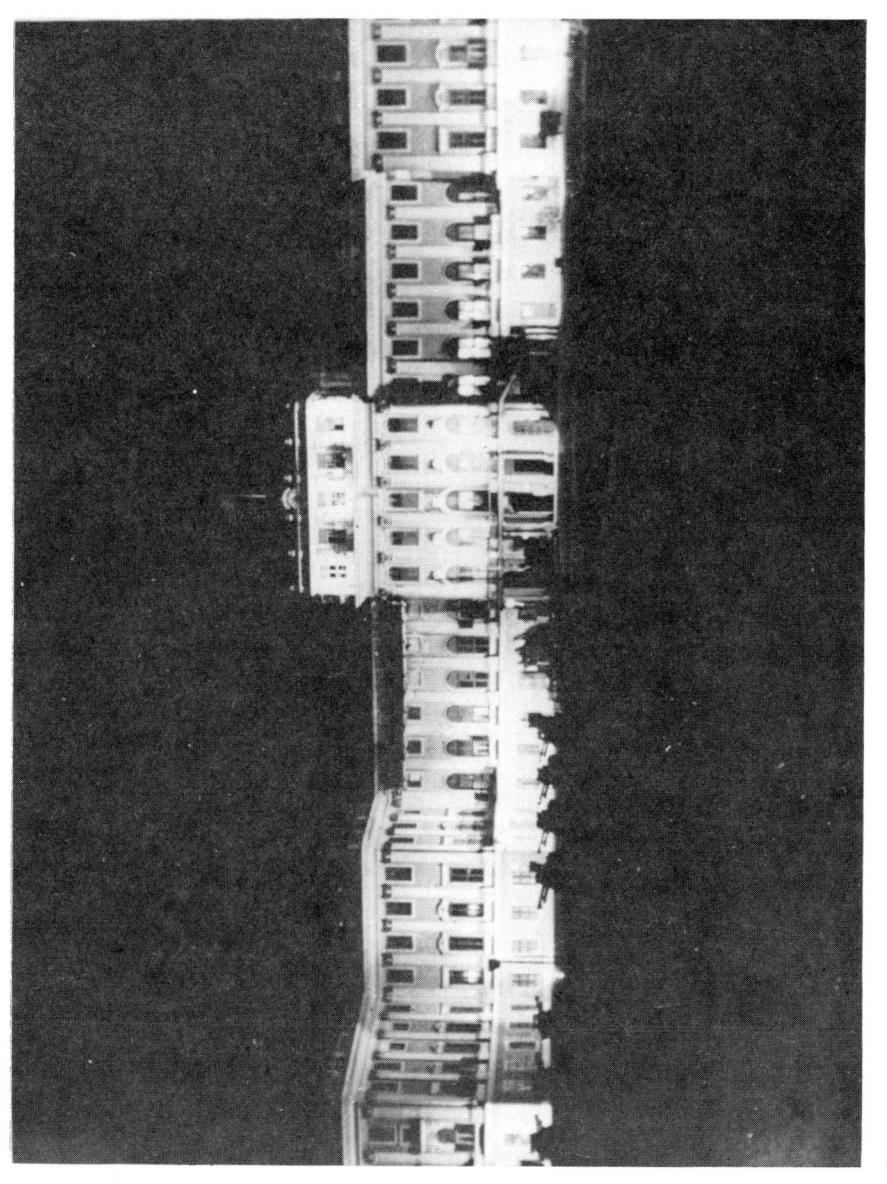

Schönbrunn Palace floodlit for a reception.

demanded that everyone should drink bottoms-up. But McCreery did not drink at all and the others following his lead, drank restrainedly.

Koniev sat back, remarking to me:

'How can we enjoy ourselves without drink? With us, we all drink, sing, eat, each one does whatever he pleases, and everyone is happy.' There was throughout the company a restrained atmosphere of exhilaration, no more. Koniev continued:

'Are you all trying to appear respectable? Is that why no one drinks? Or are you afraid to drink? Surely we are all friends here; nothing said will go further, will it?'

It was obvious that beneath the pleasant, conversational surface McCreery and Koniev were too dissimilar. Apart from their job they had nothing in common. One of our interpreters said that the trouble for us all was that McCreery considered the Russians non-Christian and therefore worthless. I explained that McCreery was a teetotaller. He held strong moral and religious principles. He was also exceptionally reserved. Koniev became thoughtful, studying McCreery's lean, austere profile. I went on to say that McCreery was very popular with the troops. He cared for their welfare and it was he who, at the dinner following their first Allied Council meeting, had proposed the toast 'to the common soldier.' Koniev nodded.

He gave up any attempt to instill a little spirit into the party. I tried to involve him in the general conversation. But he could not understand the pleasure to be got from a quiet exchange of insignificant remarks, which in translation sounded ridiculous.

He started making a point, then added: 'Oh, never mind. Scrap it'. And he turned his attention to me. 'Why aren't you married? You are obviously difficult to please. I'll find you a fiancé.'

He examined the room we were in and gave me its history. It was here that the last Austrian Emperor had abdicated. L'Aiglon had died in the next room. He knew the history of the whole Palace. I felt ashamed that I had not looked it up myself.

Renner, the acting President of the Republic, pushed his heavy bulk through the crowd of generals eating round the buffet and, unbidden, approached our table. McCreery ignored him. Renner tried to sit down between Koniev and me. Koniev pushed him aside.

'Can't the man see that I want to flirt with you?' He pulled Renner

High-Level Entertainment

down on his other side, at the same time leaning back in a welcoming manner. He poked fun at Renner who was taking his election as President for granted. Renner was relaxed in Koniev's presence. He spoke of the shooting season, saying it had just ended – shooting from now on was forbidden and he hoped the Marshal would respect the law. Koniev promised to do so. Then suddenly Renner was talking of a book he was writing on the Fourth International.

'In it I propose to demonstrate that Lenin and Stalin are traitors to the Communist cause, the cause of Trotsky.' I was stunned. To call the Head of State a traitor to a Soviet Marshal! It was with the greatest reluctance and considerable anxiety that I translated Renner's words. There was silence; Koniev stared at Renner.

He growled: 'That's going too far. . .' Then slowly, coldly he addressed Renner. As I gathered my wits in German, he stopped me.

'Oh, to hell with it! It's his seventy-fifth birthday coming up. Let the old man say what he pleases.' He smiled at Renner, who went on to describe his version of the quarrel between Trotsky and Lenin.

When Renner had departed, Koniev turned his attention back to me. He said that really I should marry a Russian, or perhaps he would carry me off himself, cossack-style on his horse. He went on joking till all at once his tone changed; he was looking at me seriously.

'And wouldn't your Press be delighted?!' he exclaimed. 'Can't you just see the headlines "Russian Marshal kidnaps British girl-interpreter"? They would all shriek "Barbarian" and wouldn't they just revel in it all? A Soviet Marshal disgracing himself!' I protested but brushing me aside he went on to say that the British Press welcomed any criticism of the Russians, especially of the military.

I insisted that he listen to me. 'Our Press is run differently from yours,' I said. 'Ours is not controlled by the government. It has nothing to do with the government, except for security. It does not reflect the official view. The Press is out to please the public and to make money. The public like sensational stories, gruesome stories. I know it is dreadful but it is the truth. They do not want straight news, not those who read the kind of papers you are talking about.' I hurried on incoherently as I was upset: 'The Press gives people what they want. No one really believes these stories. People read the newspapers as they read detective novels; the Press want a sensation

The Author in conversation with the Russian C-in-C, Marshal Koniev.

Reception at Schönbrunn Palace. Gipsy violinist in the foreground.

White Among the Reds

a day – that is their motto. It livens up the monotony of the daily routine.' Koniev had not interrupted me, but I raced on: 'In any case our journalists here in Vienna do not speak Russian, they cannot communicate with your people. They can't get to know them. But at meetings in the ACA the delegates are making friends and getting to know each other.' I was out of breath. Koniev shrugged his shoulders in disbelief. But then he smiled and touched my hand.

I told Lady McCreery quietly how deeply Koniev resented criticism of the soldiers. A little later, she turned to him and said: 'Marshal, you must be very proud of your men.'

'Why?'

'The terrific victories they won, and they never let you down.' Koniev was pleased.

'Yes, all the way from Moscow to Berlin. Not so bad!' and he started talking about the campaigns but Lady McCreery was already replying to someone else.

The dinner was followed by dancing to the music of a gypsy orchestra. I was standing beside General McCreery. Feeling rather nervous, I began: 'Marshal Koniev is upset about our criticism of his soldiers. . .' McCreery turned towards me and gave me the kind of dry smile that silences completely. I stepped away.

Koniev came up and suggested McCreery should open the ball. McCreery excused himself on the grounds of his gammy leg. Koniev said he would follow his host's example. He had probably never learnt ballroom dancing. He went off in search of a partner for me and brought back General Mark Clark. We opened the ball. General Clark was an excellent dancer and he was tall. Dancing in that brilliant atmosphere and to the strains of the highly emotional gypsy music, I forgot everything except what fun it all was. Periodically I returned to Koniev but he waved me back on to the dance floor.

As we swung round in a Viennese waltz, General Clark suddenly asked: 'Why don't you do the interpreting at the Allied Council? Our interpreters there are hopeless. We have so many unnecessary misunderstandings.'

At that moment, the Allied Council seemed very remote. I replied: 'Our generals prefer male interpreters.' He pressed my hand and we circled on.

High-Level Entertainment

As the dance ended, I found my arm clutched by a man whom I recognised as a colleague who had been high above me in the hierarchy at Reuter's, where I had worked for a time.

'Introduce me to Koniev, will you?' he begged. It was tempting for me to grant him a favour. But Koniev was a guest here. The Press might distort whatever he said and in his present mood I was afraid he might be tempted to pull their leg, and to say something outrageous.

'I don't really know him well enough,' I said. At that moment, the Marshal appeared, brushing the dancing crowd aside, hands outstretched towards me.

'I've been looking for you everywhere,' he exclaimed. 'I wanted to say goodbye.' It was an awkward moment, but I felt it was better so.

As Koniev took my hand in his firm clasp, I felt reassured and he left me in a happy frame of mind.

The dancing went on late into the night. Austrians are natural dancers, especially of the waltz, but even while whirling swiftly over the highly-polished floor, they seemed unable to resist grumbling.

'We have no freedom with the Allies in occupation. Each one pulling us this way and that,' a young official complained. I wanted to point out that here we all were, Allies, conquerors and conquered, dancing together; wasn't that a good beginning? But he was not prepared to listen, he wanted to do the talking. As we circled around together, I could not help thinking what a contribution they, the Austrians, the host country, could make towards helping us all to understand each other, if only they had the wish to do so. But meanwhile I might as well enjoy myself.

The Schönbrunn Theatre, inside the Palace itself, which had been restored was officially reopened, with a gala performance of ballet, the Vienna Philharmonic Orchestra, the Vienna Boys' Choir and finally Weingarten playing *St. Francis on the Waves*. This tiny baroque theatre created a feeling of intimacy, opulence and lightheartedness. For the first time, sitting there, I understood why the Viennese were unable to stand up to harsh reality. Everything in this theatre was light, frivolously gay and beautiful. It symbolised the character of the people.

9

Cold Living

We interpreters had been transferred into the attics of the Schönbrunn Palace. They had not yet been repaired, nor had our Mess. But with the cold in came the repair gang of Austrian prisoners of war and out came our attic windows. Chilly winds poured into the rooms, driving out those working on translations. They rushed about waving documents marked 'Urgent' and looking for somewhere to work. Girls lugged heavy typewriters around in search of a place to settle. Everyone shouted, grumbled and cursed.

As soon as the windows were replaced and we hurried back in, painting and repairs began inside. Hammering and scraping deafened and distracted us. To enter we had to climb over prostrate forms of men installing immense porcelain stoves (Our Head of Military Intelligence found a couple of Austrian prisoners of war sitting smoking inside his stove). The Secretariat chose this moment to reorganise the Interpreters' Pool with the result that some twenty civilian interpreters and translators found themselves confined to two of the small attic rooms, which also housed the telephones and typewriters. It was chaos.

As for our Interpreters' Mess, it was now considered ready for occupation. We held an official opening dinner. The house had belonged to some eccentric Count. There were fountains and stained-glass windows in the main reception room, which also had a stained-glass ceiling, its centre-piece, the bust of a voluptuous naked lady.

The Russians had taken pot-shots at her; she was riddled with bullet holes. Under her gaze we assembled.

We were a mixed lot and an odd lot. Among us were elderly professorial types and a young woman who shocked us with her low necklines. We resented all being cooped up together in this fantastic building. In spite of the generous supply of wine, we stood about in silent groups.

Dinner was served. The Austrian waiters were ancient; they wandered aimlessly around, while we waited. The food, when it appeared, was cold, the potatoes rotten; the coffee they forgot altogether. Our Mess President said a few words and we clapped politely. Then our Colonel murmured something. We had been there an hour and a half but had eaten practically nothing.

We rose in silence and transferred ourselves to the drawing-room. The atmosphere was frigid.

A young interpreter burst into the room followed by the famous Viennese gypsy orchestra. The musicians grouped themselves around the piano; it lacked a leg and had to be propped up on a chair. The next moment Strauss' waltzes flooded the room. The gloom was dispersed. We waltzed around joyfully and sipping hot wine we revelled in the stirring gypsy melodies. Some people continued to stand around with dismal faces, but they soon retired to bed.

The leader of the orchestra, a Hungarian, played the violin most soulfully; we wallowed in nostalgia. He knew and played all the tunes we requested. He attached himself to me, Vienna-fashion, and followed me around as I danced. I could not escape him. When I sat down he leant over me like a weeping willow, till unexpectedly I turned my head and dug my nose into his cheek. Janet laughed immoderately; so did the others. But the evening was a success and we felt more tolerant towards each other.

Winter came in with a great storm. A roaring, bitterly cold wind penetrated everywhere, sending bits of tile and general rubble hurtling through the streets. The creaking of rusty gutters and roofing in some of the bombed-out houses sounded quite eery. The temperature dropped suddenly. We still had no overcoats; only odd inessential items of uniform had arrived. The French were in the same predicament; their women, more clothes-conscious than we were, had been issued with men's shoes.

With no heating in the office, we crouched over our desks muffled up in every bit of warm clothing we could lay hands on. We borrowed woollen scarves, caps and woollen gloves. The YMCA, which had just opened, was a godsend. During the tea break we stuffed ourselves with the buns and cakes that they served with tea and warmed up before returning to the cold.

The nights were frosty. In the Mess, sleet and snow poured down through the holes in the voluptuous lady on the ceiling and through the broken windows. To catch it, vases were placed strategically. We ate with snow flakes settling on our shoulders. When our Colonel invited us to his room, which was heated, we dozed off from the unaccustomed warmth.

We grumbled and felt sorry for ourselves. The rest of the ACA seemed to have some sort of heating; even some of the Austrians already had, but not we. We were popular with the Austrians, we were told, because we lived in conditions similar to their own.

At a meeting of the Displaced Persons' Division which was considering the plight of homeless and stateless people, I wondered what the future held for them. I began to wonder how the Viennese were managing with their broken windows and no wood or coal. Our self-pity disappeared.

What was needed was action. In the evenings, one of us sat down at the piano and strummed energetically while the others danced; ballroom dancing, country dancing, ballet, we tried everything. We swung each other round and leapt through the air, even the plumpest and clumsiest among us; we were beyond wondering what we must look like, but at times we laughed so much we could not continue. I taught the others the dances we learnt as children, the Vingerka, the Krakoviak and the Mazurka. We pranced around as long as our legs held out, then hurried off to bed. If we were too tired to dance we sang, curled up on the couches with every available rug or blanket tucked around us. I brought a pilot back to dine with us when I heard a rumour that there was heating in the Mess; but it was only a rumour. We had to ply him with vodka to drive out the cold and

White Among the Reds

we kept him dancing all evening. Alcohol was essential to dispel the gloom of those cold evenings in the Mess.

Two male translators went for each other one night, punching and kicking out on the drawing-room floor. They knocked down chairs and tables while we pranced around egging them on like so many witches. Strange behaviour for adults, but it was demoralisingly cold.

One of them, Roger, went on strike. He stated that he was fed up and would do no more work till conditions improved. He did not appear in the office. It worked, that is, partially; a car was despatched into the woods returning with firewood and at last, although we did not get heating, the Mess had hot water.

Stoves arrived, but no paraffin. Michael Dawnay, amazed at our helplessness, produced some from his RAF Mess. He explained that in the forces each man must look out for his own interests as no one else would. But we civilians were not trained to it, nor did we know what in the forces was acceptable rule-breaking and what was not.

We had partial heating now in the Mess, but the office was still unheated so we went from warmth to cold and everyone caught chills. Strangely, we had all been quite fit when there was no heating anywhere. After a Sunday's duty in a cold, damp room I also started a heavy cold. There were now four interpreters in hospital, four in bed at home and everyone else was sneezing and coughing. Those of us not laid up were rushed by car from conference to conference.

The Austrians meanwhile strode out, skis on their shoulders, up into the hills looking extremely fit. These were the young and the healthy: still, we wondered at their robustness. We were also jealous of, and irritated by, the Austrian ladies stepping out into the streets in luxurious fur coats.

One morning, when we entered the office, we were struck by overwhelming heat – a stove was working. We had to throw open all the windows. And on the same day our overcoats arrived, long khaki ones, so stiff and heavy, with large brass buttons, that being tall, I was constantly told I looked like a Russian general. It was true that in the overcoat I could pass through into the Russian HQ without showing my pass; delegates would persuade me to enter with them so as to speed things up.

A few days later the office was again freezingly cold; a big hole

Cold Living

gaped in the outer wall. Another stove was being installed. One of our officers marched home through the streets wrapped in a blanket in protest.

I moved into the Mess and was given a large room with a balcony, a small corridor and a bathroom available also to others. It was almost a self-contained flat and it was heated. Thankfully I retired to bed and was off work for a week. We were given a maid called Christine, a cheerful and good-tempered little woman. She immediately took over and looked after me and my clothes. When the electricity failed, she carried on in the dark and when I had to wear evening dress, she would find a friend who owned an iron. She was delighted that I was confined to bed and managed to produce a hot-water bottle. Now she was able to descend to the kitchen for my food where she was offered a cup of tea or coffee, a rare treat for an Austrian. While I was ill, I was inundated with requests to explain Russian behaviour or to advise how to get the Russians to agree to certain proposals. For me this was the best of cures.

Winter was to be difficult for many people. My family wrote to say that relations of ours were stranded in Salzburg, in the American zone, and were desperate for warm clothing, food and money. There was no way of getting to Salzburg except by private car. Mr Williams, the Consul, mentioned that he was going there. I begged him for a lift. He hesitated, preferring to be on his own, but I knew he would not refuse since I was going in order to help relations; he himself was undertaking the long journey because he had heard of an elderly British lady in trouble in Salzburg. He was still 'Mr Williams' to us; we did not even know his Christian name.

The journey was to take about seven hours. I was given numerous instructions by our Colonel, who stressed the dangers of travelling around Austria and pressed his water-flask on me, though we were not about to brave the desert. Janet, her usual efficient self, prepared sandwiches and I was bundled into layers of borrowed sweaters. Off we drove, Mr Williams, his chauffeur and I with a large parcel of warm clothing that I had collected for my relations.

It was a great relief to be out of the city and in the countryside. Mr

White Among the Reds

Williams did not expect to be entertained; I felt relaxed in his company. The fields, woods, hills, all looked fresh and peaceful. We crossed the Russian zone without incident, though the chauffeur mounted the pavement several times in the villages to avoid reckless Russian lorry drivers. We ate Janet's sandwiches sitting on tree trunks in the woods.

Mr Williams took over the driving. He drove very fast and we sped up into the hills. It began to snow. Faster and thicker came the flakes; our windows were smothered and the wipers stopped working. We peered ahead unable to see much, crawling along, engulfed in all the whiteness. We were both excited, exhilarated, as we grinned at each other in the security of the car. Mr Williams was an experienced driver and managed to hold the car to the road. We reached the American zone safely and down we drove into the valley and so to Salzburg.

This was a very different city from Vienna. The streets were crowded with warmly-clad, well-shod, cheerful people. The shops stood open; the street lights shed a warm glow over everything. I understood why people here were reluctant to work in Vienna.

We drove to the British liaison officer and asked him to provide us with accommodation for the night. He was horrified. The place was full and more and more people were pouring in. There wasn't a room free. For the Consul he undertook to provide something by the evening; he would have to persuade someone out of his hotel bedroom. As for me, he drove me to the billeting officer, who looked worn out but finally, reluctantly suggested that I take over the couch in the room of a woman war-correspondent in one of the hotels. He could not ask her permission as she would not be there till the evening; it was up to me to explain the situation to her. He escorted me to the hotel and I took over the absent correspondent's luxuriously warm room and hurried into a hot bath.

Down in the dining room I walked into a miniature Tower of Babel; the room was full of officials from all over the world. I sat down at a table with an American-Ukrainian from UNRRA, a Pole, the Dutch representative for Displaced Persons and a French officer. They all started talking at the same time; it was my arrival from Vienna that had this effect on them. What emerged was their mutual

Cold Living

dread and actual fear of being sent to Vienna. I was staggered. I argued that there was nothing to be afraid of in Vienna; life was improving daily. It was useless. They had an irrational but overwhelming fear of the Russians. My pleas that the Russians had at last, for the first time, emerged in vast numbers out of their cocoon and given us an opportunity to show them a different way of life, our way of life, had no effect.

Perhaps people arriving from Vienna wanted to impress their audience and exaggerated stories of the dangers. I had noticed that those who left Vienna were often afraid to return; the Press at home frightened them more than the actuality had done. Letters were addressed to us as though we were in the front line. I tried to explain all this, but they paid no attention.

I had recently flown to London for a few days. On the return journey we ran into a storm. It was snowing hard. We could see nothing. A fierce wind tossed us around. Ice was forming on the wings of the plane. It kept dropping into space. I was very frightened. When we came down to refuel and sat over hot drinks with the crew, I told them how frightened I was. They admitted that they were equally frightened, but it transpired that they were afraid of landing in Vienna, not of the storm; their fear was of the Russians.

After dinner, I met a Brazilian war-correspondent and she helped me to make enquiries about my relations. They were away and their plight had been exaggerated. But my friend undertook to deliver the things I had brought and to let me know what further help they needed.

I now had to get back to Vienna. Mr Williams was going on to Innsbruck. He tackled the liaison officer, but was told that there was no British traffic going to Vienna. I remembered that our American friend, Charlie Thayer, had given me an address in Salzburg, which he said, would always find him. It turned out to be the HQ of the OSS (Office of Special Services). Two muscular Filipinos blocked the doorway, but when I asked for Colonel Thayer their attitude changed. I explained that he had promised to take me back to Vienna (not true, but I had to get back somehow). The Filipinos agreed to do what they could to help me. Later I received a message that one of their cars would give me a lift the following morning.

I had not seen the owner of the room; she must have come in and gone out again while I was asleep on her couch. Three American ladies, all very elegantly dressed, picked me up in an enormous car, apparently under protest as they did not answer when I spoke to them nor did they share their packed lunches with me. I went hungry. But I got my own back at the Russian frontier. When the driver got out to show his pass I heard the Russian officer checking the documents ask: 'And who is that in the back?'

His sergeant replied: 'Only his women.' We were not required to show any documents. I translated the sergeant's words for the benefit of the ladies; they saw nothing humorous in the remark!

And so back to cold Vienna. I quickly repressed a slight hint of apprehension and told myself firmly that I was glad to be back.

10

Marathon Conferences

The Allies were caught up in marathon Four-Power conferences which dragged on without a break for five, six or even eight hours. Delegates sighed, speech slowed down, they were exhausted. The meetings were without apparent result. At one conference I interpreted Russian alone from five in the evening to two the next morning. I could no longer remember what my delegate or the Russian had said; I had to refer back to each continually. The Russian delegate apologised for 'exploiting' me and added: 'but you interpreters are making a great contribution to our common cause.' A meeting of the Economic Directorate lasted from five in the evening to one in the morning, resumed again at half-past ten that morning and went on till two in the afternoon. One French interpreter instead of translating his delegate's words into Russian started rephrasing them into more elegant French; his delegate thanked him for improving on his French. After these meetings at night I turned over and over in bed willing myself to unwind; I had to get sufficient sleep before the next day's conference.

The Western Allies blamed the Russians. It was some time before the Russians let drop any comments. The first to do so were Colonel Ilichev and Lieut-Col. Miasnikov of the Internal Affairs Division. After preliminary discussions had lasted all morning, thoroughly exasperated, Ilichev mumbled:

'They are all too long-winded, especially the French. They talk too much. And why must they make literary essays of their reports?' Seeing my eagerness to hear his point of view, he went on to accuse us of spending hours discussing mere details; we were too much attached to form, to traditional, out-of-date methods of coping with problems; we used jargon which could be understood only by lawyers, doctors or financiers; we overloaded, over-complicated everything. General Morozov, the Russian Chief of Staff, had said something similar – that we British were fettered by our traditions and conventions. The Russians and the Americans had more in common, being young nations, prepared and eager to adopt new methods.

On policy, when the meetings would come to a final halt, the Russians remained silent. It was Brigadier Block, the Head of our Internal Affairs Division, who provoked Ilichev into speech. The meeting had been arguing over an appeal for help addressed to the whole world and launched by Austrian religious organisations and the Austrian Red Cross. It was in the style of 'Save Austria! Save her Music!' The Western Allies approved the appeal, the Russians disagreed. There was deadlock.

Brigadier Block broke the silence: 'We should really find out about Austria's priority of claim as compared with other countries.'

The normally reserved, monosyllabic Ilichev burst out:

'Austria fought against us! You forget that! And it is we who are now responsible for her! This appeal condemns the Occupying Powers, that is ourselves! They are asking to be saved from us!' Startled, the other delegates wondered why they had not previously seen it in that light. The appeal was refused. The Brigadier had unleashed a torrent of pent-up bitterness.

As the delegates prepared to leave, Miasnikov stopped beside my chair, leant over and hissed into my ear:

'It's disgraceful! That Austria should appeal to the world when others are suffering so much more! If it were Belgium, Holland, France or Leningrad, they would have our whole-hearted approval. But Austria! Austria has no idea what suffering means. They haven't seen what I saw in the Ukraine, children with stomachs swollen like balloons from starvation. They didn't see the Leningrad women and children under artillery fire, crossing the frozen lakes to escape the famine.' He caught his breath, and continued: 'And they dare talk of rape. Then why do their girls walk about the streets alone, after dark, loitering and asking for trouble? They squeal to the world for help and at the same time show off their fur boots and their wonderful fur coats!'

Colonel Ilichev with a brusque gesture pushed him aside and leaning over me announced: 'You know what we ought to do? March the whole lot of them on foot through the snow to Stalingrad and back!' He banged his clenched fist on the table: 'That would teach them what suffering means!' He paused, then: 'I hate and despise the whole lot of them! To hell with them! And they aren't even trying to work!' Calming down, his face lit up with eagerness: 'Why don't you come to Russia? Come and see how our people work. Come and see what efforts they are making to get life back to normal!'

At meetings Ilichev continued to criticise the Austrians: 'They expect everything to be done for them, while they sit back and complain. And do they ever show any gratitude?' Then shuffling his papers unnecessarily, he suddenly said: 'I know what people are saying about our soldiers. We have taken strict measures against those guilty of misconduct. Among so many men there are sure to be a number of criminals; one can't expect soldiers to behave like angels.' I said that on the whole the soldiers were behaving decently enough. We lapsed into a strained, painful silence. Our Press was still raking up sensational horror stories about the Russians of which the Russians were well aware, just as we knew the contents of their newspapers.

Ilichev and Miasnikov had agreed at another meeting that for soldiers to fire into the air whenever they felt like it was both disgraceful and highly dangerous. It must be prohibited. Ilichev nudged Miasnikov and his face for once all smiles, whispered: 'Remember how we all fired into the air? When peace was declared? It was on the East Prussian front,' he explained to me. 'It was our immediate reaction. We started firing and all the soldiers followed suit. That really was stupendous!'

I listened to the Russians but I never asked questions; the Russians never questioned me either. It was an intuitive mutual understanding. The infamous NKVD (now called KGB) inhibited us. The NKVD was an army in itself, responsible for internal security. Under Stalin it had grown into a kind of monster internal spy system. It was safer

White Among the Reds

never to give the Russians information which they might be required to pass on. It had become a habit never to ask questions. I gave it no more thought.

I was immediately suspicious when a certain Lieut-Col. Kuzmitsky began to question me at a meeting of the Health and Welfare Branch. He accompanied the two regular delegates supposedly as a specialist on epidemics. He pranced up to me, addressing me by my Russian patronym, his face stretched into a set smile and asked where I had learnt my Russian. I did not know him and I disliked the familiarity. Neither of the two regular Russian delegates spoke to him and I noticed that they were avoiding him. He had to introduce himself. I took the hint – NKVD – and my whole being shrank from him; it was a physical feeling of repugnance.

At lunch after the meeting he sat down beside me, edging his chair nearer mine and saying he wished to 'have a talk' with me. He asked when I left Russia, where I was born and so on. I slid my chair as far away from him as possible and professed ignorance about everything – I was too young to remember – at home we never spoke of the distant past – we were British and had no connection with the Soviet Union. He switched to Russian art and literature. He was well-informed but I made no comment. He mentioned Hungary, where he had been stationed. He called it one vast black market where anything could be bought in any currency. There was scorn in his voice. I marvelled that in such a despicable profession a man should retain scruples. At last the meeting ended. I dreaded having dealings with members of the NKVD.

There was an NKVD officer once in General Morozov's quarters. I had called on business and strolled into his ADC's office. Usually the young officers sprawled, relaxed, in the armchairs, smoking and joking. Now they were on their feet, their dress in order, their faces serious and withdrawn. I was asked formally what I wanted. I then noticed an officer standing at the window, his back to me. On the desk lay his cap with the significant red band of the NKVD. I delivered my message and hurried away.

The only other NKVD officer I came across was a Major-General Fomin. He had a frog-like appearance with a broad, flat face, great big ears and great big hands. He aroused in me the same instinctive feeling of repugnance. He and Col. Tappin of the Allied HQ in Italy were signing an agreement on the repatriation of 13,000 Poles from the Second Polish Corps in Italy. The new Polish government did not believe that we were repatriating all the Poles who wished to return and they suspected us of holding back Polish war criminals. So after the agreement was signed, General Fomin tried to get permission for a certain Polish Major Czarnecki to visit the Polish Corps in Italy and investigate these suspicions. We were reluctant to let him come. Fomin led Col. Tappin aside into a corner of the room and whispered to him that he need have no fear of Czarnecki's being a . . . here he bent conspiratorally towards me, cupping his massive hand behind a prominent ear, as though eavesdropping. He implied a spy. It was a vulgar, distasteful gesture.

After the meeting Col. Tappin and I drowned our disgust in wine over lunch. Tappin said that if this Major Czarnecki insisted on visiting the Polish Corps there was no guarantee he would come out alive. The 13,000 Poles returning home had had to be segregated from the others to protect them from being molested.

Our Intelligence people came up with an extraordinary rumour – that Col. Ilichev was the head of the NKVD in Vienna. I could not believe it. He seemed so direct in his manner. I did not get this 'NKVD feeling' with him at all. The French head of the Internal Affairs Division, the Prefet Maljean was suspicious of Ilichev and Miasnikov. He kept repeating that I must never trust them. Ilichev he accused of being a counter-espionage agent and Miasnikov of having been dropped as a secret agent in the UK during the war; the Prefet was convinced Miasnikov only pretended not to speak English. It was true that when British officers were negotiating to get their Russian wives out of the USSR, it was to Ilichev that they were directed, in most cases successfully. But did that necessarily mean he was NKVD?

I repeated the Prefet's suspicions to Mr Nott-Bower, our Chief of Police. He shook his head in disbelief saying that in any case whatever Ilichev and Miasnikov might be, we had nothing to fear. We had nothing to hide. He would like to show them and the French all over Scotland Yard, as neither of them had any idea of a non-political

White Among the Reds

police force, and there they could see one in action. The more the Russians heard and saw the better.

Yet the Prefet Maljean himself once allowed me to drive off into the night alone with Ilichev and Miasnikov. I was with our Supervisor of the Austrian elections. The Russian Supervisors were Ilichev and Miasnikov. The Prefet Maljean represented the French.

After hours of waiting for results in the Inter-Allied Secretariat, our British Supervisor decided to watch the counting of the votes in the Town Hall. He suggested the others join him. Ilichev protested that if they, that is the Russians, so much as showed their noses they would be accused of improperly influencing the voting. Our Supervisor left but the others decided to remain where they were so I had to also since without me they were unable to converse.

We played cards (Russian Fools – the Russians have a passion for this simple game) till the early hours of the morning and saw the first two results come in; in the American zone a communist was elected, in the Soviet, a conservative. The Americans and the Soviets joined in the laughter. Since there were no more results, the Supervisors decided to leave. My delegate not being present, Ilichev offered me a lift home.

I cursed our delegate for placing me in this predicament. I expected the Prefet to find an excuse to stop me going alone with the Russians. It was one thing to hold certain views, but quite another to have to stake one's life on them. But the Prefet unconcernedly prepared to leave, as did the American. I had to accept.

We drove off into the night in a Soviet car with a Soviet soldier at the wheel, imprisoned between two supposedly NKVD officers. I remembered the number of times Russians had told me that I should return to my country, and just how invaluable I would be there; I remembered all the jokes about carrying me off by force. There was nothing to be seen outside the windows. Just blackness. I had no way of knowing where we were going. I hoped my chatter sounded natural.

The driver braked, sprang out and opened the door. We were outside the Interpreters' Mess. How gratefully I thanked them for bringing me home! It was only later that I realised they had not enquired and I had not told them I was living in the Mess.

Marathon Conferences

A highly prejudiced, self-opinionated, anti-Russian friend of mine on meeting Ilichev saw nothing sinister about him. Dr Scott asked me to arrange a meeting with Ilichev. He wanted permission to deliver penicillin to a children's hospital in the Russian zone of Vienna. Scott was a brusque, outspoken man. He was not working in the Commission but giving medical care to Slav refugees in desperate straits. They were hiding in the countryside fleeing from the communists. He was full of tragic stories and hatred for the Russians. All the way to the Russian HQ he held forth against them though he admitted he had never actually met one.

Ilichev and Miasnikov came forward to greet us in the friendliest manner. We sat down and Ilichev asked: 'What can I do for you?' Scott explained. He spoke frankly, expressing his concern for the children and appealed to them for help. To my surprise he addressed Ilichev as he would a friend who, he was sure, would respond positively and Ilichev did. Scott was given the permission he sought. He proceeded to shake hands with both the Russians many times over. He came out smiling, and at the door, turned back again, to thank them once more. As we drove back, he was thoughtful. There was no more raving against the Russians.

With Kuzmitsky and Fomin it was obvious what they were. But Ilichev? The hard-headed Dr Scott had taken a liking to him.

The Russians assumed that we were also watched by our internal security police and that political blunder could cost us our jobs and our freedom, as I realised on another occasion.

The same Dr Scott persuaded me as a favour to interpret at a meeting of nurses. Our British delegate was a long-faced, mannish hospital matron. When our transport arrived, climbing into the back, she motioned me to sit in front with the driver. She looked formidable; the driver's company was preferable. At the meeting, she barked out orders at me, without a 'please' or a 'thankyou'. I fumed inside, but carried on interpreting. At lunch the matron motioned me to sit at the side-table with the driver though as a result, the delegates were unable to converse. As the driver had no qualms about asking for second helpings, he and I tucked in with relish.

The Russian delegates, two doctors and a nurse they were introducing, were at a loss how to treat me. They cast frightened and

White Among the Reds

compassionate glances in my direction. They presumed I was in the kind of trouble they dreaded for themselves. They did not speak to me and when I interpreted for them, they kept their eyes on their documents.

The Russian nurse was a gentle young woman with an enchanting oval face; she was very shy. She had probably been chosen to represent Russian nurses as much for her looks as for her nursing skills. Dr Talanov, the chief delegate, kept thrusting her forward, talking about her devotion to duty, of the compassion shown by Russian nurses and their self-sacrifice. Our matron's thin lips clammed shut; she had come to the meeting to hear facts, not praise. Talanov went on boasting of the excellence of Soviet medicine, nurses, doctors; it was out of character and foolish. I wondered whether my supposed demotion had affected and confused him. We drove back, with me once more beside the driver and no 'thank-you' from the matron.

A difficult problem for us Russian-speakers were the requests we occasionally got from Russians, searching, they said, for their lost relatives abroad. We never knew whether they were genuine requests, or those of agents-provocateurs, trying to find out our attitude towards their own traitors. Only once did I agree to search for a relative of a Soviet officer, but my efforts in any case were unsuccessful.

At the next meeting of the Health and Welfare Branch, on seeing me re-instated in my usual favoured position, the Russians said nothing, but they kept patting my arm and smiling at me.

I went with Scott and two other British doctors to the last concert of the Schweshnikov choir. The tickets had all been sold, but two Russian lieutenants, whom we met outside, produced four free tickets for us. The choir was magnificent. Scott's face was alight with pleasure. At the end he rose to his feet with the rest of the audience, clapping and shouting: 'Bis! Bis!' The crowd carried him down the aisle to the foot of the stage where the choir were singing encore after encore. I hoped Scott would remember that evening and I wished our Press for a change would report on such a scene.

The agony of the long meetings was suddenly lifted when catering was laid on in the Inter-Allied Secretariat itself. The Ally presiding for the current month (they took it in turns to preside) was to be responsible for providing the food and drink. We started with drinks at mid-morning, then progressed to lunches, then dinners. The Allies began to vie with each other in producing the most lavish buffets – caviar versus salmon, every conceivable kind of salad, ham, cold meats, all were spread out before us. Vodka, cognac, wines and whisky flowed in limitless supply. We ate, we drank, we ate and we drank. Day after day. The Russians proposed toasts, starting with 'The Ladies!' Each toast was downed in a gulp. It played havoc with the interpreting but the delegates were beyond noticing. They sat flushed and grinning, occasionally mouthing their words. Sometimes it was difficult to stay awake. Recriminations ceased. Misunderstandings seemed very amusing. Everyone had become so charming. One of our delegates drank eight vodkas at one sitting. He beamed at us, his long red nose shining prominently. The Russians were soon saying 'OK' and the Westerners 'Ya Soglasin' (I agree). General Miachkine, the Russian Air Force Chief, enticed our Russophile Air Commodore to a buffet-luncheon. Giving me an encouraging push in his direction he whispered: 'Come on! Do your stuff. I want him for a friend.' I presented the Air Commodore with vodka after vodka. Soon Miachkine's arm was round the Air Commodore's shoulders and they were laughing.

We all over-ate and drank too much, but we interpreters considered it worth while. Agreement became the rule rather than the exception. But not in the Executive Committee and the Allied Council where meetings remained decorous.

A senior member of the Inter-Allied Secretariat entered a conference room once unexpectedly; a Russian girl interpreter was dancing on the table, the rest of the meeting were standing round it, singing the tune with 'tra-la-la' for words and clapping out the rhythm. After that sobriety reigned once more, but only for a short while.

The American delegate transported the entire Internal Affairs Division to the Baroch Club, a select night club for senior American officers, where pink lighting and red upholstery created an intimate atmosphere. We dined there, danced and drank. Ilichev was persuaded to demonstrate the Russian dance. As our old friends the gypsy orchestra launched into it, he took to the floor, spread wide his arms, made a few tentative steps, then with a burst of embarrassed laughter hastily withdrew. Miasnikov tried to dance cheek to cheek with a Russian girl interpreter. She pushed him away. I heard him assuring her that this was customary in the West and it was right for her to conform. She refused to listen to him and left the dance floor. Our host an American colonel launched into the jitterbugs, just then coming into fashion. In spite of his grey hairs, he was extremely agile; his whole body jiggled up and down rhythmically, his legs and arms whirling around wildly. The Russians looked on in amazement.

It was puzzling that although we all left the meetings – it must be admitted – tipsy, the agreements reached were never rescinded, so why were we unable to reach the same agreements when sober?

11

Life Returning to Normal

Life in Vienna was gradually becoming more normal with the Allied forces merging into the Vienna scene.

Trainloads of Austrian prisoners of war arrived daily from Soviet captivity. First came the maimed; they were young and cheerful. The girls hurried to bring out the finery they had kept concealed; they blossomed out and became elegant. In the Opera it was almost like pre-war days except that we continued to shiver with no heating.

With stricter discipline enforced incidents, though still occurring, were of a less serious nature. Our people accepted them more philosophically and at times were even able to see the comic side.

Two drunken Russian soldiers forced their way into the Officers' shop in the Kinsky Palace (the Palace had been taken over as a dinner-dance club for British officers). The Russians grabbed the till; the young Austrian assistant behind the counter clung on to it. Two British officers buying socks there appeared not to notice anything unusual. This was too much for the Russians; they let go of the till and ran away shouting: 'To hell with the lot of them!' The British officers later explained their behaviour by saying: 'It was none of our business.'

And then stories began circulating about our men also, about the two drunken British officers who demanded a 'night-duty tram' and when a tram was produced ordered the driver to take them up the hill to their Mess.

The local population were less terrified of the Russian soldiers now that they constantly rubbed up against them in the streets and in the shops.

There was even talk of Soviet soldiers being badly treated by their officers, and sympathy was expressed; they were said to work very long hours, to have nowhere to wash and no-one to look after them when they fell ill; they slept on straw. Some Austrians showed kindness towards them.

Olia, a Russian interpreter, and I were buying Christmas cards when a convoy of Mongolian troops crunched to a stop outside the shop. Very young-looking soldiers leapt down off the straw on top of the lorries and onto the icy snow on the ground. In their great-coats, fur caps and ear flaps, they looked like Teddy Bears; they had rifles slung over their shoulders. A group followed us into the shop. They huddled together in the corner, very shy, and watched what we did. I looked over some cards, chose a few and handed the money to the shopkeeper. After some nudging and whispering, one fellow was propelled forwards to the counter. He copied what I had done, looked over the cards, picked out a few at random, and handed them with his wallet, stuffed full of paper money, to the shop-keeper. She took a note out and handed the cards and the wallet back to him. She then handed him the change. But I had not been given any change; he hesitated, the coins lying on his open palm. The shop-keeper smiled, picked them up, put them in his wallet and pushed the wallet into his coat pocket. The soldiers all ran out, laughing noisily, into the open again.

The cold was piercing. An old lady, an Austrian, appeared with a Thermos flask of hot coffee. While she stood smiling in their midst, the soldiers passed it round and then returned the empty Thermos with grins, shakes of the head and thank-yous in a language I did not understand.

But they were tough, the Soviet soldiers. Our commiseration was wasted. On a night so cold that our cheeks froze, we drove past a Russian sentry outside a Russian establishment fast asleep on a chair, his overcoat flung across its back. Afraid that he might freeze to death, we stopped. Our driver shook him awake and helped him on with his coat; the soldier nodded his thanks. When we drove on we

Life Returning to Normal

saw him climb out of the coat, fling it over the chair, sit down and go back to sleep.

In this bitterly cold weather, Russian officers and soldiers passing through Vienna expected to find shelter wherever they knocked. They complained that the Austrians did not accept them into their houses. We explained that the Austrians were afraid of them and afraid for their possessions. Possessions, the Russians parried, are not as valuable as a man's life. In Poland in winter, they told us, in spite of their presence being bitterly resented Polish peasant women opened their doors at night and invited the soldiers to sleep in their huts.

One Russian soldier forced his way past the guard and into one of our Military Police posts. The astonished MPs watched him calmly bedding down on the floor. They seized him and were about to fling him out when Colonel Gordon-Smith, our Deputy Commandant, walked in. He spoke Russian and took in the situation. He explained to the MPs that to throw the man out on a freezing night would be a most uncharitable act in the eyes of the Russians; the MPs would have to accept him for the night. They let go of him; the soldier lay down on the floor and immediately fell asleep.

I came in contact with Soviet soldiers when occasionally I volunteered to go to the Russian Commandatura for Soviet newspapers. The sergeant in charge of the library was a neat, angular man. The first time I came in soldiers crowded round me and wanted to look at the miniature wristwatch I was wearing. They all begged me to exchange it for anything in their possession. I knew what a passion Russian soldiers had for wrist watches and it was stupid of me to wear such a valuable one on this job. One man grabbed my wrist. The sergeant intervened.

'Now lads, no rough manners. Leave her alone.' They obeyed him.

One soldier strolling in asked: 'Got a spy story?'

'No,' the sergeant answered.

'Anything to read?'

'No, nothing.' The shelves were crammed full of books by Lenin, Stalin and other communist literature.

Another time, a very drunken soldier appeared. Clutching the door, he made his way unsteadily round it, felt along a bench, sat carefully down and gave a loud hiccough. The sergeant apologised.

White Among the Reds

'Please excuse him, Comrade. It's our holiday; we are celebrating. Better come back another time.'

I found the Russians normally considerate of our feelings. A Russian soldier lay on the pavement. As I approached, I heard an officer tell a passing sergeant: 'Cover him up. The Allies don't like to see dead bodies.'

But social manners presented a problem for the Russians. Their officers employed in the ACA were normally well-mannered and smartly uniformed, but they did not always know how to conform to Western custom.

After a dinner given by General Winterton, our Deputy C-in-C, for General Zheltov, his Soviet counterpart, Zheltov took an orange. Mrs Winterton sliced hers in two and began eating it with a spoon; Zheltov unobstrusively returned his orange to the bowl. I had also taken one; it took me some time to interpret Winterton's scowl and to put mine back too.

General Morozov, the Russian Chief of Staff, marched in to a meeting, then with a quick gesture cupped his chin in his hand. During the luncheon that followed there were two tables, one for the senior members of the meeting, the other for the interpreters and the ADCs. When my neighbour had to leave our table, General Morozov slipped across and sat down in his place, mumbling:

'It's very boring at the other table.' He still had his hand round his chin. I could not help peering at it.

'Well, what are you staring at?' he demanded. 'If you must know I haven't shaved. All right, I know it's disgraceful, but stop staring.'

I said that since he had joined our table it was up to him to entertain us.

'How?'

'You could tell us a funny story.'

He told what he considered a funny story.

'So, what is funny?' I asked. Morozov did not answer. His ADCs looked fixedly at their plates. I began repeating the story to the others who did not understand Russian, to see whether they thought it funny. Morozov stopped me. When I repeated it later to Janet, she explained and laughed at my stupidity. I had not understood because

Life Returning to Normal

it had not occurred to me that Morozov would tell a vulgar story in public.

A Russian officer whom we had taken with us to dine in the Kinsky Palace, after a couple of drinks began gesturing at the conductor of the orchestra and asking him to play tunes he knew. He started singing them loudly. He was not drunk, just relaxed and enjoying himself. We were getting very cold stares from a group of Air Force officers, but there was no stopping the Russian. When these officers rose slowly to their feet and advanced in a group towards our table, we whisked him rapidly away.

In their uniforms Russian officers looked handsome, but they were keen to show off their new western-style suits, which they were now allowed to wear off duty in the evenings. In the theatre we hardly recognised them. Major Kovalev, the liaison officer, looked vulgar with padded shoulders and a tie clashing with his suit. The girls too, charming with their fresh faces and natural manners, looked gaudy when they wore make-up. We heard that these girls were attached to Russian officers to prevent them from being attracted to western girls. It may have been true in some cases, but I hoped not.

It was the Soviet National Ensemble of Folk Dancers that made the Russians more acceptable generally. They gave a superb performance and introduced Russian folk dancing to the West. The girl dancers were so very feminine and graceful, the men so masculine. There was so much vivacity and humour in their dancing. To-day these Russian dance groups are famous throughout the world, but for the two hundred British guests there that night, it was the first time they had seen anything like it. We had a delegation of Members of Parliament visiting Vienna, and they were also invited. The audience loved the whole performance. Many of our people stood up and crowded the aisles to get a better view. They would not stop clapping and the performers had to repeat their dances over and over again, though they were sweating and must have been exhausted.

I had been invited by Ilichev; I sat between him and Miasnikov. They watched me and my colleagues and seemed to doubt that our pleasure and admiration were genuine. They kept repeating: 'Do they really like it?'

They had probably invited me to sit with them so as to be able to judge for themselves whether I really enjoyed the performance. I certainly did. They promised that more singing and dancing groups would be brought to Vienna for special occasions. But what an inferiority complex lay concealed beneath their official boastfulness!

As I left Ilichev told me that I was always welcome to any Russian performance and should I not receive an invitation, I was to let him know. Also that they could always provide the necessary transport. I took this as a tribute to my famous great-grandfather.

The Russians were also past-masters at chess. Many of our officers enjoyed a good game with them. In the Park one afternoon I met Monsieur Goldet, the French head of the Economic Directorate, who invited me in to tea and a game of chess. I was a moderate player and he beat me easily. I happened to mention this to General Morozov. He was shocked at the lack of gallantry on the part of Monsieur Goldet and that same evening dropped in on him, demanded a game of chess, beat him and came away satisfied and reported to me what he had done.

I was keen as we all were to establish Austrian contacts. I managed to trace Hacker, an Austrian refugee, who had worked with me during the war at Reuter's, in London. Now in Vienna, he was editor of the *Socialistisches Korrespondenz*. I invited him to dinner. He turned up very pale and gaunt. Another friend, Karl Heiser, from the USA Health and Welfare Branch came round that same evening. I invited him to stay on too.

At Karl's we had once had an embarrassing evening with an Austrian Minister and a woman worker from the Austrian Department of Social Services. The two Austrians had immediately weighed in against the Russians. Karl, resenting these constant attempts to set the Russians and ourselves against each other, unconsciously slipped into the stance of the conqueror. This led the Austrians to adopt a servile attitude, the attitude of the vanquished. It stopped all reasonable discussion.

With Hacker things went differently. Karl and Hacker were both engrossed in politics. Both were idealists. They felt able to speak frankly to each other and each got what he wished off his chest. Karl

Life Returning to Normal

was bitter about the Austrians, about their grumbling, the way they lived in luxuriously appointed apartments and accused the Russians of having looted 'everything'. They constantly whined that they were hungry, yet Austrian doctors assured the authorities that health generally was good and that there were none of the usual epidemics.

Hacker was critical of the Allies. He resented the way we lumped all Austrians together.

'You can't judge Austria as a whole; you have to judge each political party separately. They are all aiming at different goals, they are all pulling in different directions. But you Allies, you just lump us together and then condemn the lot.' Hacker had been dropped by parachute behind the enemy lines and had fought on our side. There was nothing servile about him.

When he was leaving, Hacker refused to accept the packet of tinned food I had prepared for him.

He invited me to the theatre. We spent an Austrian evening, that is without supper and without transport. We watched a rather dull play, the acting very stylised, in a cold theatre. But afterwards we talked at length though across an empty table. I tried to explain how irritating the Allies found this Austrian negative attitude of constant complaint. As host country to the four Allies and in close touch with all of them, could they contribute nothing towards keeping the peace, the peace that we felt was so precarious? Could they not help to overcome the differences between East and West? Geographically they were ideally placed. They should be able to understand both sides. We were all sitting on a volcano and the Austrians were stirring it up. Did they really want an explosion? Had they no suggestions for helping?

Hacker appreciated my frankness and promised to pass on what I had said to higher authority.

The next morning I received a huge bouquet of flowers from him.

For some Austrians the future held only tragedy. The landlady of some of our officers begged me to help an artist friend of hers; he was in serious trouble as he had appeared on a list of Nazis. His name was Karl Schwetz. I had seen postcards of his etchings displayed all

White Among the Reds

over Vienna; he high-lighted the more romantic, old-world corners of the city. I agreed to see him on the following Sunday.

In came a delightful old gentleman, dressed in a kind of frock-coat with a high stiff collar and a bow tie. He was clutching a portfolio which he proceeded to drop; his etchings scattered over the floor. We scrambled about collecting them, then sat down somewhat breathless. It was a very cold day; all I had to offer him was gin. He was delighted. He sat sipping it, savouring it in silence. Probably he had not eaten for a long time and I have no head for hard liquor. Soon we were grinning at each other companionably. As Karl Schwetz eagerly accepted gin after gin I wondered whether he would be capable of taking his leave.

Because his name, he told me, was found on a Nazi list, he had been put to hard labour and he was afraid for his hands. He spread them out; they were calloused, swollen and already deformed. He understood nothing of politics and had no idea whether he had or had not been a Nazi; he only cared for art. It seemed futile and tragic to put such a gentle innocent on to such work at his age and in midwinter. And it was painful that he should have to come begging to me in this way. We both needed that gin.

He showed me the etchings. It was a new Vienna I saw; graceful, elegant, rich in life and feeling. The detail was exquisitely drawn. Karl Schwetz beamed as he gazed at his own work. I undertook to sell his etchings to my fellow interpreters; this would raise money for him.

He managed to leave with dignity. With the gin inside him at least he looked warm and was smiling.

The Austrians were each allocated a minimal ration of food daily, depending on their needs, that is on the job they were expected to do, so one no longer came across starvation. But once as I was returning to the Mess, I saw a man lying in the road. Austrians passing by were paying no attention. He must be drunk, I thought. When I leant over him, he murmured something. I made out the word 'wasser' (water). I touched his shoulder. His eyes opened and he whispered over and over again 'wasser' and 'hilfe' (help). I was able to lift him up but he kept falling from me; he had no right arm and he felt like a skeleton. I managed to get him into our Mess hall and called the guard to bring a chair. He sat stiffly straight, staring ahead, saying nothing. I brought him water and then soup with some bread crumbled into it. He was reluctant to accept it, then swallowed it slowly in silence. I questioned him.

Finally he mumbled that he had no means at all; he had lost his arm in the war. That was all he would say. He must have been wandering in a semi-conscious state till he fell down. Our servants kept away from him – a Nazi – otherwise he would have received his ration of food and would have been given some kind of job.

When he was sufficiently recovered, I asked our army driver to take him home. Our military cars were not allowed to carry Austrians, but he agreed to do so. I offered the man some tins of food. He ignored them. He would not give his address, but our driver whispered to me:

'Don't worry. Once I get him away from these servants and the guard, he'll tell me where he lives and I'll see he takes the tins. It'll be OK'

It was horrible to know that for this man there could be no hope, no future. When I had asked him whether he had any relatives, he had answered: 'Who would want such a relative?'

12

The Commandants

Our British Commandant, Brigadier Palmer, was leaving Vienna. An Inter-Allied farewell party was held in his honour in our Military Mess. Among the guests were the new Russian Commandant, his deputy and their wives. General Blagodatov, the former Russian Commandant, had been relieved of his post; it was rumoured because there had been too many complaints about the lack of discipline among the Russian garrison. A tougher man had been brought in. He was Lieut-General Lebedenko.

Lebedenko was a heavy man with a fat face and a purplish, bulbous nose. He could always be located by his loud snorts. His lady was like the Russian wooden dolls with round, red cheeks and big, round eyes.

As soon as the Russian party arrived, they were placed in my care. Lebedenko's lady felt obliged to explain his snorts: 'He will smoke much too much.' That was her only verbal contribution for the evening; she just sat bolt upright and displayed her handsomeness.

Mr Williams, the Consul, appeared. He was all smiles and invited me to dance; I loved dancing and there was no one with whom I enjoyed it more. He told me his name was Alan. In between dances we returned to the Russian group. Alan Williams assured me he enjoyed their company. I repeated to him all that was said.

General Lebedenko was a silent man but his deputy, Major-General Travnikov, revelled in talk. He was a small, cheerful person with a

Brig. Verney, Brig. Palmer and Col. Gordon-Smith.

welcoming, friendly manner. He plunged into speech without reservations expressing all that was in his head and his heart, his gestures as expressive as his words. I introduced Alan as our Consul.

Travnikov turned to me: 'But diplomats are all liars,' he cried, horror on his face. 'They are cunning, unscrupulous. You should keep well away from them, have nothing to do with them. They don't know what truth and honesty mean.' I assured him that Alan was not like that; he only concerned himself with Consular affairs. Travnikov shrugged his shoulders, smiled and shook hands. I translated what he had said, but Alan laughed and remained unperturbed. He never expected people either to hold views similar to his or to conform in behaviour. He accepted and respected people as they were. I had never before met anyone completely unprejudiced. It forced me to reconsider my own attitudes.

Travnikov explained that he had never had anything to do with what he called 'diplomacy' before coming to Vienna.

'Now here, I'm completely at sea; I can't cope at all. I'm no longer allowed to attend meetings of the Commandatura because I blurt out the truth. So, thank God, I only have to deal with the army. That's my kind of work and I understand it'. Blagodatov and Palmer he labelled 'diplomats' and said they were 'cunning', but Lebedenko: 'He always puts his foot in it, and what a foot!' True enough Lebedenko had massive feet. Travnikov went on: 'All your officers are "diplomats". They all know how to conceal their thoughts and their feelings. Their gestures are restrained and their faces without expression. In fact, one wonders whether they have any feelings at all!' He laughed.

'When I first met the British I assumed they would all be haughty, like Richard Lionheart. I read a book about him; he's the only Englishman I know anything about. But here in Vienna I find Englishmen are not at all like that.' He smiled approvingly at the noisy, friendly company.

Then he paid official tribute: 'The Normandy landing was a classic achievement in history as Stalin has stated.' Russians felt the need to quote Stalin from time to time as some kind of reassurance. Dropping this formal manner of speech, he told us how, at the time, his troops were bogged down and demoralised. When he got the first signal

The Commandants

about the landing, he did not know whether it was the real thing or whether it was successful, but he ordered all the loud speakers to blare out the news: 'The second front is opened; the Allies have landed on the European continent.' Scouts carried the news to all outlying posts and leaflets were dropped to the guerilla groups. 'You can't imagine what an effect this had on our men. They were jubilant!' He expressed appreciation for the British and American military equipment sent to the USSR: 'Until we got this equipment, my eighteen thousand men at Rostov only had three hundred rifles between them.'

On what front had the General fought, Alan asked. He had commanded an infantry division at Stalingrad. He described it:

'We were beaten; Stalingrad had fallen. We withdrew further and further towards the river, till it cut off our retreat. Desperately we dug in along a stretch of some twelve kilometres in length, and only six hundred metres in depth. There we were trapped underground, beneath the battered buildings like so many rats. The C-in-C was fifty metres from the Divisional Commanders; these were 50 metres from the Battalion Commanders, who were right in the front line. Of my original twelve thousand eight hundred men, only six hundred remained. And my wife, my dear wife, she was there with me.'

His arm was round her waist; he drew her to him. She was a most attractive slightly-built young woman with natural, unaffected manners. 'She was a Stalingrad Film Star before the war,' he said with pride. 'She refused to leave and stayed underground with me. A shot nearly carried my leg off; we had no medical help; but for her it would have been all up with me. But she nursed me and saved my leg.' He held her tighter and she smiled in his embrace. 'But we knew it was the end; we waited to die.' He was silent for a while, then continued: 'Our radios were promising all the time that we would be relieved, telling us to hold on but this was, we realised, just patriotic talk. Then our Siberian scouts – they can slip through anywhere – returned from reconnaisance and reported that over long stretches the river was enveloped in an enormous smoke screen and that they had seen huge concentrations of troops on the other side. It was of course nonsense. Nothing could save us now.

'The roar of a massive artillery barrage behind us from across the river suddenly shook the buildings above and crashed into the German positions beyond. We were deafened, stunned, buried in the debris, but these were our guns, our men! It was incredible! A miracle!'

General Travnikov held up his glass and emptied it in one go; his wife was watching him anxiously. He announced that he needed another drink and started pushing his way through to the bar. She clutched my arm and whispered:

'He's not allowed to drink; it's his leg. You must stop him!' As I looked doubtful, she continued firmly: 'If you don't, I shall start screaming. I will!' She opened her mouth, her eyes determined. I hurried after the General, took his glass out of his hand and filled it with soda water. He was taken aback, then laughed.

'My wife, I suppose?' I nodded. His wife had only sipped at her glass but she now confided to us with surpise that she felt slightly dizzy.

We joined the central group of officers where General Lebedenko was addressing Brigadier Palmer. He said that soldiers knew what trifles often led to war so they were sure to come to an agreement, but politicians who fell out simply threw the problem back at the soliders to be settled by fighting. He stopped, then grinning added that Brigadier Verney, who was taking over from Palmer, would have to unravel many of Brigadier Palmer's entanglements – with the ladies – especially in about nine months' time. He wagged a fat finger at Palmer, who flushed angrily. Lebedenko hastened to assure him that he was only joking. He brought out of his pocket a Russian silver cigarette case with a troika engraved on it – a farewell gift to Palmer who now blushed with pleasure. The Russians crowded round him, slapping him on the back and shaking his hand. His weakness had won their affection.

So it was with Brigadier Block, Chairman of the Internal Affairs Division. He had once appeared at a meeting in green corduroy trousers instead of his usual immaculate uniform. The trousers caused a sensation; I explained to the Russians that he had attended an ATS ball the previous night which went on till five in the morning. He was exhausted and had dressed as comfortably as possible. They were delighted. As they left, they kept repeating:

'Well, good-bye dear Block' (the 'Brigadier' was dropped for good).

Russian and French Commandants, Generals Lebedenko and Du Peyrat.

White Among the Reds

They shook his hand over and over again and Block in his usual way asked:

'What's it all about now?'

Brigadier Verney had become the British Commandant. He invited me to the Opera with his deputy, Colonel Gordon-Smith, a large man with an ugly face and a most engaging smile. We saw the *Fledermaus*. General Lebedenko was present sitting bolt upright in a box, a famous singer from Turkmenistan at his side. She had a clear creamy complexion, a broad, animated face, a magnificent carriage and thick black plaits reaching to below her waist; the audience gaped at her. During the performance I realised I had forgotten to bring a handkerchief and my sniffs began to accompany Lebedenko's snorts till Verney handed me his handkerchief.

Over dinner after the performance, Col. Gordon-Smith and I began to pontificate about the Russians. In our eagerness to explain their conduct we kept interrupting each other and raising our voices till we suddenly realised there was no need to explain, we were saying the same things. I was excited; it was rare to meet someone who understood the Russians better than I did and who obviously cared as much as I did. It was heartening and it gave me confidence. We felt like old friends after a long separation. I had noticed the high esteem in which the Russians held Gordon-Smith; he treated their senior officers with the respect due to their rank regardless of circumstances or appearances. Later I learnt that Gordon-Smith had a Russian mother but he concealed the fact, things Russian being suspect particularly among the military.

A Guards Regiment had arrived in Vienna. Gordon-Smith told us that on New Year's Eve when trouble was expected as the soldiers poured out drunk from their barracks, four of our Guardsmen immediately got into a fight with four Russians. These were astonished that the Guardsmen were prepared to fight it out though they were unarmed, whilst our men were amazed that the Russians, so much smaller, managed to hold their own. By the time they had more or less knocked each other out, they piled into a bar and together started getting drunk all over again and pulling the bar to pieces as they drank. When finally arrested they marched arm-in-arm to the police station bellowing at the tops of their voices. Lebedenko was so delighted that for once the trouble was caused by our soldiers acting together, instead of against each other, that he proposed allowing them to sleep it off and then letting them go scot-free.

Brigadier Verney listened to us and made a suggestion that Col. Gordon-Smith and I should dine with him regularly once a week and discuss local problems. I accepted eagerly. He had a tough job.

Alan Williams and I received a standing invitation to the Military Mess weekly dances. He picked me up and we spent the evening dancing together and chatting with the Russian group.

The next time General Travnikov greeted us as old friends. He told us about the chaotic early days in Vienna:

'The Russian is a peaceful, lazy creature. He can stand a lot, but once roused there's no stopping him. You can see that for yourselves right here in Vienna! There's no controlling them though we are doing our best.' Complaints poured in of the abominable behaviour of Russian troops in certain parts of the city, so he decided to investigate. It was Sunday and he was wearing civilian clothes. He went to the cemetery that had been pointed out to him as the centre of trouble. He found a soldier behaving disgracefully – he did not specify what the soldier was doing – and started rebuking him, whereupon the soldier turned on him shouting:

'You get the hell out of here!' He and his companions started towards him. 'I was helpless; I ran. Never again did I go out in civilian clothes!'

At the height of the battle for Vienna Cardinal Innizer sent word to say that his Palace was being plundered by Soviet soldiers and would Travnikov do something about it. One of his colonels seized the first two soldiers in the street and ordered them to accompany the messenger and supply whatever help was needed. Unfortunately he had picked on two bandits who robbed the Cardinal's messenger and disappeared.

'Do you think the Cardinal believed us that we had not done this deliberately? But there was such a mix-up; many of our men looted German stores and put on German uniforms as their own were falling to pieces. You can imagine the confusion!'

This brought him to the subject of deserters. Sighing deeply, Travnikov complained that deserters were causing endless trouble. We reminded him that at the meeting that very morning, the Soviets had denied that there were any deserters. He waved this away nonchalantly, saying:

'Of course, officially, we have to deny it. There shouldn't be any, quite true, but these deserters, they keep turning up all over the place, behaving appallingly and ruining the reputation of our soldiers. One man, dressed in Red Army uniform, travelled all the way up here from Moscow. Said he had come for loot! Everything had been taken from him on his return home, so he had come back for more. And another problem are the orphans. They are turning to gangsterism as we haven't managed to round all of them up yet.'

He started talking about the renegade Russian soldiers who had fought for the Germans, saying that we were still concealing many of them in our zone. He was silent a moment, looking at me steadily. These cossacks would probably be shot if we handed them over. I pretended to know nothing about them. Then I felt ashamed at deceiving him. He changed the subject not wishing to embarrass me.

All this time a rather uncouth captain, officially an interpreter, kept close to Travnikov's side, listening to all he said. It worried me, but the General chatted on unconcernedly. I hoped he knew what he was doing.

He went on to tell us about General Vlassov, the Commander of the renegade Russian forces. Vlassov has been his friend and companion at the beginning of the war. They fought together in the defence of Moscow. Then he went over to the Germans.

'Can you imagine it! Going over to the enemy! Fighting against your own soldiers!' His eyes were angry. 'I didn't believe it! I couldn't believe it! His troops were more cruel than the Germans; they took no prisoners. Incidentally, this helped with the morale of my own men; they had been deserting in whole groups. Now Vlassov's ruthlessness caused them to pull themselves together. They realised their families would be treated mercilessly by Vlassov's men.'

They captured Travnikov's Chief of Staff and tortured him. Travnikov claimed that he had seen the body and had immediately given the order that all prisoners taken that day should be shot there and then. Travnikov told us that Vlassov was captured by an advance party who caught a captain on his staff. The man promised that if they did not shoot him, he would lead them to Vlassov's HQ. So by night they stole forward and entered his HQ where he slept, capturing him and his staff. They were flown to Moscow where they were now awaiting trial.

Alan was dancing with Travnikov's wife. It was hot in the Mess. Every so often, she disengaged her hand slightly from his and blew from a distance into her palm to cool it. She did it most elegantly, but it was embarrassing for Alan. When they rejoined us, I asked the General what he expected to do when he left Vienna. He was silent.

'I won't get promotion,' he said finally.

'Well, tell them why,' his wife insisted. 'Admit it! Go on, be honest.'

Travnikov looked embarrassed: 'Well, before the war, I was the leader of a gang of bandits on the Volga.' We were stunned into silence, then we all started laughing. 'I don't mind about the promotion. Major-General is good enough for me,' he added.

Col. Gordon-Smith and I both believed that if you won't drink with the Russians they assume that you do not trust them. We had instilled this into Brigadier Verney.

At the end of the Russian Presidency, he and three other officers from the British Commandatura received invitations from General Lebendenko to dine, with their ladies, in his house. This was the first time Lebendenko was entertaining. Brigadier Verney asked me to accompany him.

Knowing that Verney would offer us drinks first, I had a few titbits to eat beforehand. Verney, foreseeing heavy drinking with the Russians, prepared a whole dinner. When we arrived at Lebendenko's we found a banquet laid on.

We queued up to greet our host. He sat enthroned on a kind of dais, his huge body overflowing, looking the image of Pushkin's brigand, Pugachev. The young woman, who accompanied him to the Military Mess dances, sat on his left, a massive elderly lady on his right.

'Whom do I greet first?' Verney was intrigued.

'Commandant, wife, mistress,' I advised. We greeted them in this

White Among the Reds

order, then mingled with the crowd. Soldiers playing concertinas strolled around as the guests took their drinks. Sentries stood at attention with rifles fixed at the doors. I happened to mention to one of the British officers that most Russians are good dancers; they learn it in their villages. He wondered whether this was true of the soldiers there. I approached one of the sentries and asked whether he would dance for us. He smiled shyly.

'I don't mind, if the others do too,' he replied.

The musicians formed a circle and broke into a rhythmic Russian tune. The soldiers leant their rifles against the doors, tightened their belts and gave themselves a little shake as though to loosen their clothing. The next moment they sprang nimbly on to the floor, crouching down, their backs straight, hands to the waist, shooting out their legs one after the other. They whirled, pranced, flew through the air – each lad dancing to his own fancy. One soldier, a little apart, gyrated slowly on the tips of his toes; he was a gypsy. It was a delightful interlude.

We sat down about a hundred guests. Lebedenko took his place at the head of the T-shaped table with the Turkmenistan singer, Tamara, and her husband. At his side stood his Chief of Staff, General Komarov, staring ahead, aloof from all the proceedings. A chair was placed for Lebedenko's wife but most of the time she hovered behind him. Down the length of the table Verney was the first guest on Lebedenko's right, with me beside him, the American Commandant General Lewis facing us and the French Commandant, General Du Peyrat, next to me. The other officers sat according to rank down to the end of the table.

The table itself was laden with dishes worthy of a feast: enormous platters of roast meats, hams, chickens, pâtés, caviar, cheeses, every variety of salad, enormous bowls of fruit, every conceivable delicacy and bowls of flowers everywhere.

'I suppose this is the whole meal?' Verney ventured. I supposed it was. So we set to. Waiters bustled round refilling glasses of vodka and cognac for the men. We ladies were given wine and were left to sip it at our pleasure. Lebedenko started the toasts: to the Allied victories in war, to co-operation in time of peace. Then General Komarov proposed the toast to our host. Others countered with

The Commandants

similar themes, downing in one vodka and cognac alternately. Verney noticed General Lewis emptying his glass into a potted plant. He tried to do the same but Lebdenko cried shame on him. General Du Peyrat was pouring his drink onto the floor.

Lebedenko beamed with delight at having his friends around him, but it was on Verney that he centred all his attention; he could not take his eyes off this elegant, handsome figure, by far the most distinguished-looking officer present. Lebedenko was thrilled and flattered that Verney should be his friend, drinking with him here in his home.

Lebedenko had long ago given up any pretence at eating and we had all eaten our fill; the dishes were being cleared away. Lebedenko now launched into toast after toast. His wife, hovering anxiously over him, kept popping bits of food into his mouth as soon as he opened it.

'Woman, leave me alone!' He pushed her away.

'But you must eat. You're drunk!' she pleaded.

'Get back! Can't you see, this is the first time they're in my house. We're all friends here. What does it matter if we're drunk?' She shook her head, smiled at me and shrugged her shoulders.

Verney, sitting very erect, more dignified than ever, began to stumble over his 'esses'. A glassy look crept into his eye. He asked whether he really was obliged to drink any more. I had to admit that Lebedenko would be very disappointed if he did not keep up with him.

'Well, here goes,' Verney announced, downing his twelfth vodka.

Doors were flung open and a procession of chefs entered, each bearing a hot dish, which was carried round, displayed and placed on the table. Verney turned to me reproachfully, and to my dismay I saw he was squinting; not only was he squinting but I had never before seen eyes looking straight across each other, quite like that. He murmured that he must get out; he couldn't take any more. People had been leaving the table and returning, so I suggested he slip out into the garden for a while. He rose with great deliberation, swayed a little, but managed to get safely down the length of the table and disappeared. But almost immediately he was back, saying that machine-gunners had insisted on escorting him into the garden and

White Among the Reds

he had not fancied remaining there with them, so they had all marched back in again.

He plunged once more with grim determination into the round of toasts, vodka, cognac, vodka, cognac. Lebedenko's face was now puce. As we ploughed through the hot dishes, a host of entertainers poured into the room engulfing, as it were, the lot of us. Groups of dancers swung around, singers gave forth lustily, acrobats climbed up and down each other forming human pyramids, jugglers balanced hoops while others leapt through them, a band played folk tunes at one end of the table and we could just make out an orchestra at the other end playing chamber music. Tamara, who was called 'The Star of the East' rose to her feet and began swaying voluptuously over the generals. Her face came closer and closer to that of General Du Peyrat and her cheek lightly touched his. He raised his arm and brushed her aside as though she were some kind of fly; the noise, confusion, heat and general chaos was too much for him. Undismayed, Tamara continued swaying over the others. We pressed her to sing something in English; she apologised for her 'Eastern' accent and sang Tipperary. It was all straight out of a Russian fairy tale.

Then Lebedenko waved a hand, General Komarov barked out a command. Doors opened and out came the Austrian kitchen staff in their white aprons, headed by the chefs in their tall white hats. They lined up against the wall. Such was the exotic atmosphere, that for one hideous moment I wondered whether they were all about to be shot. But Lebedenko merely raised his glass and mumbled:

'To the authors of our banquet, we say "Thank you!" ' We all raised our glasses and the kitchen staff were each given a glass of champagne.

Finally Lebedenko rose to address the company. There was silence. The entertainers withdrew; the waiters disappeared. He leaned heavily on the table and mumbled something about: 'My friends . . . very honoured, humble home . . . everything yours . . . now peace . . . very happy.' His interpreter rendered a more coherent interpretation. Lebedenko collapsed back into his chair calling loudly on Brigadier Verney to reply.

Verney stiffened, hauled himself to his feet, more regal than ever, and whispered: 'Say something – go on!' I also rose and stood close to him as though listening to what he was saying.

'Mr General,' I began. Then in desperation I repeated more or less the speech I had made for General Morozov. As I reached the end I remembered that Lebedenko belonged to a Guards regiment so I concluded with the words:

'So, Mr General, as one Guards officer to another Guards officer . . .' Before I had time to finish, Lebedenko was on his feet, shouting: 'Yes, Yes! That's it! We are brothers-in-arms, both Guards officers! And as the highest tribute one officer can pay another – you shall have my Guards badge!' He plucked his breast but found he was not wearing it. Turning back he tore the Guards badge off General Komarov, who never moved, and gripping the table, made his way round and pinned it himself on to Verney's jacket.

Verney murmured: 'I couldn't have asked for more . . .' and they both flopped back into their seats, while everyone rose to applaud and began to disperse.

Verney sat, his head in his hands, looking greenish. He murmured: 'I've had one too many. Go away.' As I left with General Lewis, he was amazed how Verney could stand up to it all and how composed and elegant he still looked. Evidently his condition was not obvious to others. 'Amazing man!' Lewis exclaimed.

There was dancing in the hall and it was cooler. I decided to persuade Verney to join us there; then he would not have to drink any more, but as I returned to the table Lebedenko lurched towards me, arms outstretched murmuring: 'My little heart!' I hurried back to the dancing.

Finally we decided with the other officers that we could, in all decency, now take our leave. I went back to Verney; he was sitting very straight, his eyes glassy, and solemly he announced: 'The worst has happened . . . both Lebedenko and I . . . together . . . under the table.'

We got him away and though swaying dangerously he continued to smile fixedly. He even patted some junior Russian officers condescendingly on the shoulder. Descending the stairs, he managed to return the salutes of the soldiers on guard. Finally we drove away leaving one officer to hunt for Gordon-Smith who had not been seen

White Among the Reds

since he left the table half way through the banquet. Verney fell asleep in the car.

Bang! The car swerved and stopped. A hole, the driver told us, had been pierced in one of the tyres – presumably by some Austrian trying to cause trouble between us and the Russians. The Russians would not do such a thing to their own guest. There we were in the middle of the night, stuck in the centre of Vienna and the Commandant drunk.

Leaving Verney with the driver who was given strict instructions not to open the door which we locked, the other officers went in search of another car and I went with them. They stopped one, commandeered it and drove it rapidly back to Verney.

The driver was standing at attention in front of the door, saluting smartly and shouting: 'Yes, Sir! Certainly, Sir! Straight away, Sir!' while inside a furious Verney battled with the door handle, threatening him with savage punishment.

Verney and Gordon-Smith were rather shamefaced when we next met. Verney had only a hazy recollection of events after the hors d'oeuvres. Gordon-Smith had collapsed in the washroom, he told us, and woke up in his own bed, in his own night clothes with no idea how he had got there. Verney had stayed in bed the next day. General Lewis had not been seen for several days. When I next met Lebedenko he enquired whether Verney had got into trouble, and admitted, with a chuckle, that he had been reprimanded for drunken behaviour and had had to keep to his quarters for five days. It was not clear whether as a punishment or out of necessity.

Verney was afraid he must have been very drunk. I told him that Lebedenko would have been most disappointed and humiliated if he had got drunk alone. Verney was puzzled and a bit worried by the Russian Guards badge on his jacket. When I told him how it had got there, he was thrilled and very pleased with himself. He said: 'So, was I . . . er . . . all right?' and I answered: 'You were magnificent!'

13

Trips with Alec

I accepted eagerly any invitations from my friend, Alec, of the Intelligence Corps to accompany him on any of his trips. Civilians living under military administration were at a disadvantage. The military knew how to obtain transport, arrange trips, get passes. We didn't.

Snow had been falling steadily but our skiing was restricted to short runs on the slopes of the Schönbrunn Park. Alec was arranging for a lorryload of Intelligence people to travel to Veitsch, a skiing resort, for the week-end. He invited my friend, Olia, and me to join them.

The countryside was unrecognisable. It was cleared of rubble, the people looked more robust, they strode along cheerfully and this in the Soviet zone where life was harshest; it was the area where most of the fighting and bombing had taken place. The Austrians we came across had an innate dignity; they were mostly young country folk, wounded ex prisoners of war who thanked God they were beaten and that there was peace.

The drive to Veitsch took three and a half hours. Now we had to climb up the mountainside, skis on our shoulders, carrying our food and our belongings. We set off bravely enough. Very soon my shoulders were blistered and bruised from the rubbing of the skis, I was breathless, my calf muscles ached and the snow was getting deeper and deeper. Olia sat down; she felt sick; she could not go on. I was glad of this excuse to turn back, but one of the guides offered us his father's hut half way up the mountainside quite near to where we had stopped. When we accepted he and Alec decided to stay there with us.

The cabin backed onto the forest. In front the snow lay untouched, its surface sparkling in the sunshine and stretching cleanly away down the hill. There was not a sound except for gusts of wind in the trees; we stood awhile still and silent.

Having brushed the snow off our boots and trousers we lit a big fire in the stove and cooked lunch. Olia remained resting while Alec and I followed Sepp the guide up through the wood. Sepp chose what he called easy slopes, but we crashed into every tree within reach, till finally Alec actually skied up into the branches of a large tree! Sepp doubled up with hysterical laughter and the somewhat formal relations between us broke down. We extricated Alec. He was quite proud of himself; never before had he heard of anyone skiing up a tree. We were obviously not made to be ski champions.

When it became too dark we returned to the hut. Sepp prepared a meal by the light of the fire – we had no other. We ate squatting in the warmth of the stove while he told us of his life as a soldier in Holland and Russia. He had been wounded many times; his thin, wiry body was criss-crossed with scars, but he was a cheerful young man.

He told us he had decided to show the girls in a Russian village how to do their hair more glamorously. They covered their heads with shawls or pulled their hair back into a tight bun. He washed a girl's hair, curled it and she looked so attractive that all the other girls clamoured to have their hair done too. He spoke of the villagers with warmth and affection.

That night Olia and I squeezed into the single bunk where it was warm. Alec and Sepp climbed up into the attic. They had a bunk each there and according to Alec they lay frozen and sleepless.

We woke to find Sepp had already lit the stove and tidied up. He was waiting impatiently for us to get up as the porters and guides came to the hut to warm themselves on their way up and down the mountainside. First to appear was Sepp's father; he was followed by a stream of men who had to be fed mugs of hot tea. Higher up, they told us, there was dense fog making it dark and very dangerous.

Trips with Alec

It continued to snow all day long. Olia skied around the hut, collapsing she said every few yards. We climbed higher up into the woods on skins. It was difficult going up, the slopes were steep. Sepp said that the guides climbed them with weights of thirty kilos on their backs. We saw one skier, bent double, trying to climb up and sliding slowly backwards down the hill, shouting: 'But I *have* skins on!'

Sepp shouted back: 'Yes, but they're on upside down!' We skied back through the gaps in the woods, but invariably Alec and I disappeared among the trees and a loud crash followed, with Sepp shouting:

'Alec! Masha! Wo sind sie dann? (Where have you got to?)' We were tangled up in our skis and sticks and the branches of the trees; Alec's glasses were smothered in snow. We were weak with laughter.

In the evening, the father brought us two candles – this was to thank us, Sepp said, for feeding his son. We hugged the stove, played cards and welcomed in the New Year with hot wine. It was freezing hard outside; the wind whistled shrilly, eerily around the cabin. An enormous moon threw the shadows of the fir trees on the snow like great black fingers reaching out towards the cabin. Lowering his voice Sepp told us that mountain monsters were said to creep down these finger-shadows and grab their victims. Men had disappeared and were never seen again. Their souls, lost and wandering, could be heard wailing, demanding proper burial, but their bodies had never been found. He fell silent. The candles flickered, the wind rose into a loud screech, cold draughts crawled up our legs. Olia and I huddled closer together. Alec got up grinning and refilled our glasses.

Sepp began telling our fortunes. In the cards he saw meetings, friendship, affection, tenderness and love.

'He's falling for you!' Olia whispered in Russian.

'Falling for both of you,' Alec commented. 'Can't make up his mind on which one to settle!' So we talked on, mostly light-hearted nonsense. Olia was a cheerful person who never took things too seriously.

The sun was bright in the morning and the frost hard. Our companions appeared skiing down from the top of the mountain and we joined them. The run down was easy – even Alec and I managed it comfortably. Olia crashed into a tree, hurt her leg and had to walk.

Back in Vienna we felt rejuvenated and ready to tackle work again. Olia was not badly hurt though she had to be taken to hospital for an X-ray.

Alec was sent on a mission to Prague for a few days. He offered to take me with him as his interpreter. He knew very well that I did not speak Czech, but as it was a slack period I agreed to go. He asked me not to mention the trip to anyone, so I sent a message to the office saying that I was unable to work for the next few days, hoping it would be understood that I was unwell.

I never questioned his activities. He once told me why he had agreed to do Intelligence work. He believed the more we knew about the Russians the more chance there was for peace and better relations. It was important to discover the true state of affairs. We could then avoid misunderstandings which might lead to serious trouble between us.

We set out in a jeep, a soldier driving and all wearing uniform. Alec was armed with a sheaf of important-looking documents – the passes needed for the journey. It entailed travelling through the Soviet zone as far as the Czech frontier.

I had often driven within the Soviet zone with Alec. We called it 'swanning', traipsing around the countryside with only semi-official approval. I thought nothing of it. He wore the Intelligence badge on his cap and I took it for granted our trips were strictly legal. He produced the required documents and the sentries let us through. We picked up Russian soldiers, gave them lifts and chatted with them. Alec's grinning face and natural welcoming manner made them feel at home. It was a pleasant way of getting the information required.

Not that it was always necessary to enter the Soviet zone to pick up information. There was a panic on once, as Russian tank forces were reported to be advancing on Vienna. Alec was instructed to find out whatever he could about them as quickly as possible. He walked out of his office and into the park, happened to meet me, we strolled along together and there, advancing towards us, was a Soviet officer with the tank insignia. Alec offered him a cigarette; we settled down on a bench and they began talking. The officer mentioned that several tank regiments were on manoeuvres, these would last two weeks and he gave the name of their Commander. Alec returned to his office and received official congratulations for producing such important information so promptly!

This time at the check point leaving Vienna and entering Soviet territory, Alec was detained a long time in the Soviet guards' hut. I could not see what was happening. He came out at last pale and sweating, clutching his papers. He told the driver brusquely to get moving, which was unlike him.

'Are you all right?' I asked. He nodded and we drove off.

He had been scared, he admitted weeks later. The sentries had been suspicious of his documents, although they were covered with the usual important-looking seals. He also admitted that we had no passes. We never had had. He made up the documents himself, faking signatures. This was the first time a sentry had queried them. Most of the men could not read. Had I known this at the time, I would have been terrified, travelling through the Soviet zone illegally and with forged passes!

We gave lifts to Russian soldiers. Alec's beaming countenance set them grinning as they scrambled on board. They were sick men mostly, whose wounds had reopened and they were making their way to the nearest hospital, in some cases twenty or thirty miles away. All were excited at meeting English people and riding in an English vehicle. Some were overwhelmed with emotion and speechless. The usual collection of looted articles hung from their belts, making it difficult sometimes for them to squeeze in. They freely admitted it was loot and we were very welcome to anything we fancied. The soldiers were shabby, rather dirty and in their heavy overcoats most cumbersome, but with their cheerful, comely faces, they were good to look at and we found them pleasant and interesting company. They had the good manners of country folk; they shook hands all round, including the driver; they shared their cigarettes with us and, those that had any, shared their drink. When Alec offered them a cigarette, it was stowed away. One man apologised saying:

'When the folk back home see this, they'll have to believe that I really did meet an Englishman!' Another man pleaded: 'Could you give me something more solid? Something that will keep for sure till I get home?' Alec gave him the whole packet of Player's cigarettes.

At times there were one or two men in the back and sometimes a whole crowd of them squeezed in. Alec put his questions and they willingly told him which army unit they belonged to, who their commander was, where they were stationed and anything else he wished to know; they were eager to oblige.

When there was time a general discussion started up. What were we fighting for during the war? One soldier said that he had fought for his fatherland.

'What do you mean by your fatherland?' Alec asked. After a moment's thought he replied: 'Our village with the birch tree above the stream and the old folk cooling off outside in its shade.'

Only one man, an officer, refused to answer a question. He replied to several, but when Alec asked who his commanding officer was, he hesitated, then announced that this he was not allowed to divulge and that an Allied officer should know better than to ask such a question of another Allied officer. But left us with a smile and wished us a pleasant journey.

We asked one soldier when he would be going home. 'When Stalin gives the order,' was his answer. They all showed complete faith in Stalin.

Our driver sat silent, obeying orders, taking everything in his stride, without smiling or showing any interest. A gang of particularly rough, unshaven soldiers, clumsy in heavy fur coats, all got up at one and the same time in the restricted space at the back of the jeep and started pushing each other about. They were trying to express their thanks, to clasp our hands, and to climb down. There was pandemonium. The driver then made his only remark:

'Funny, aren't they?'

At the frontier the Russian guards refused to let us through. The sergeant was literate; slowly he read out what was written on the pass: 'To the frontier,' which he pointed out, we had now reached. The next pass said and he read it aloud: 'From the Czech frontier to Prague.' But there was no pass for the neutral zone – some thirty yards – between the two barriers. Alec was exasperated. They argued for over an hour. Finally Alec asked me to complain that as a friend

Trips with Alec

of Marshal Koniev I hardly expected to be held up in this manner. Reluctantly I did as he asked. It worked. The barrier was lifted and we drove on. By this time, a queue of British army lorries had formed up behind us. We wished them luck with the sergeant.

This was my first trip in Czechoslovakia; vast fields, stretching away to distant forests, no fences, everything open; neat villages with stone huts painted red, pink, green, blue and yellow; the people looking placid and smiling, the military looking very smart. When we reached Prague we had travelled nine hours and were exhausted.

Life-size portraits of Benes and, to our surprise, of Stalin dominated the hotel entrance hall. There was no room for Alec; he had to stay at the British Mission, but we had supper in my hotel, a proper meal with real butter.

We went sight-seeing the next morning. Prague was a city of silhouettes. Its grey-green domes, steeples and spires, some round, some square as if their tops had been lopped off, rose up on all sides, stretching towards the sky. There were no tall buildings to obscure or dwarf them. So slender were some of the spires, they seemed to drift into the sky. We strolled through the wide streets and across the numerous squares till we reached the river Vlata flowing through the centre of the city. We hovered on the famous Charles Bridge, with its statuary depicting dramatic scenes from the lives of Saints. We had no guide book. It was fun guessing the meaning of their gestures and it was fascinating to watch the crowds hurrying past indifferently beneath the enormous arms outstretched above their heads in vivid action, some in blessing, some in supplication.

The people were well-dressed, quiet and restrained in manner. They so resembled the Russians, that at any moment we expected them to throw off their reserve and turn into the unruly, expansive Russians of Vienna. At one moment, a car hooting wildly rushed towards us. Alec exclaimed: 'Sure to be Russians!' and it was. Russian military were rarely to be seen. The army of occupation had withdrawn. We had witnessed this withdrawal as it passed through Vienna. Soldiers came riding through the town perched on the top of cars and springing on to others when the car branched off away from their route. The tops of lorries, carts, everything that moved was teeming with soldiers. It was a terrifying sight, but we never saw an accident.

We were stared at wherever we went. The only British in Prague at the time were about six officers in the British Mission.

A student persuaded us to attend a ball that evening at the university. It was for the law students who were receiving their degrees. Several thousand people were present all in evening dress, the girls in long white gowns and carrying bouquets. It seemed like pre-war days. The professors, their ladies on their arms, marched in procession up onto a stage. The students gave an exhibition dance, which was followed by general dancing. Fat Mamas lined the walls round the hall, gossiping and proudly pointing out their daughters to each other.

Our uniforms attracted the students, who formed a circle round us. This gave Alec an opportunity to question them. He mentioned that the country seemed to be drifting rapidly towards the Soviet Union and communism. Was this what they really wanted? Yes, and they explained that though culturally they belonged to the West, the West had proved itself unable to defend them. They did not blame the West; geography was against them. So they, the Czechs, had no alternative. For their own protection, they were forced to ally themselves with the Soviet Union. Alec asked:

'Isn't this a drastic decision to take? Aren't you afraid?'

'We're Slavs too. We know them,' a young man replied. 'The Soviet occupation wasn't all that bad. Their soldiers went wild the first few days. But we know how to handle them. We showered them with flowers, food and drink. We celebrated with them. Our womenfolk we hid. What we lost, didn't matter. Once the first wild celebrations were over, they behaved reasonably enough. Certainly it was a relief after the German occupation.' They all agreed. They were calm and resigned about the future.

We went round the shops the next day. They were full of articles made of glass and all sorts of knick-knacks and costume jewelry. Prices were reasonable. Only food and clothing were rationed. We dropped the vowels from Russian words – that is how Czech sounded to us – and the shopkeepers understood us.

Alec took me to tea with another Czech student, a musician, whom

Trips with Alec

he wished to interview. The student told us how his father had spent the war in a Germal gaol. He himself had been carted off to a labour camp, but had jumped out of the train and cut his wrist open. He had been very ill and was incapable of doing any hard work. He was only twenty-one now. He played the piano for us while we had tea. Alec discussed the future with him. He also believed that the Czechs must join the Russian block, so that in the future they would have Russian protection.

That evening we saw *Sarka* by Filichov at the Opera. The singing was good and so was the orchestra, but Alec could not stop laughing because the heroine repeatedly clutched her middle, singing: 'Moi zhivot! Moi zhivot!" meaning in Czech: 'My life! My life!' but in Russian it meant: 'My stomach! My stomach!'

We caught a fleeting glimpse of Popski in his black beret leaving the hotel in his jeep – 'swanning', as usual. He was sure to turn up in unexpected places, and I regularly translated protests from the Russians on his illegal entries into their zone.

Having spent the two days in Prague, we started back. We picked up two Czech soldiers. They sat perched on the edge of the car seat, their faces red, their hands clenched. In reply to our questions they grunted and looked confused. They were clean, neat and disciplined, but they had been taught to 'know their place'. Alec was an officer; they were unable to relax in his presence. They and the Russians were fellow-Slavs, but what a contrast between them.

The jeep quickly filled up with Soviet soldiers once we were across the frontier. They shook our hands lustily and talked loudly. One round-faced youth gripping my hand in his two, exclaimed:

'Never will I forget this great moment in my life, when I met you Britishers!' Another inspected everything in the jeep, including ourselves, feeling and prodding, even fingering Alec's army buttons. He then thanked us profusely saying he was sorry to be so inquisitive, but it was the first time he had met anyone English and he wanted to remember everything about us. I remembered Gorki's remark on his return to Russia after a trip to America:

'How good it is to be back in Russia, where everyone of us is crazy!'

White Among the Reds

At the meeting of the Internal Affairs Division the next day, Ilichev, the Russian delegate, asked me to my confusion:

'Did you enjoy your trip to Prague?'

14

Talking to the Russians

Every Russian loves to talk yet how difficult conversing with them had become. The great barrier was language; speaking through an interpreter was stultifying. We few Russian-speakers were the only people able to talk to them, but opportunities were so few. ACA Soviet members were only allowed to associate with us at work or at official functions and even at these, conversations were discouraged. The Soviets realised that their manners were not socially acceptable in our society, that their people lacked training in discretion, that only their defects were considered noteworthy by our Press, so the less they were seen and heard by the Allies the better – such had become their attitude.

For the Russian officers not part of the ACA or of the local garrison, there were no such restrictions so far. So we valued every opportunity to talk to them. I felt I now knew Russian taboos, I had more confidence and they reacted with less suspicion.

'Man is a strange animal; never satisfied. The more he accumulates, the more he wants. Perhaps it really is best to own nothing,' a Russian officer mused. We had picked him up in the bar of the Sacher Hotel. He had strolled in, taking it for a public bar and was about to be evicted when we claimed him as our guest.

He looked about forty, was almost bald and stooped badly (from serious wounds, we later learnt). He was in fact twenty-five, he told us. He was the son of an actor in the Komisarzhevsky Theatre. Before

White Among the Reds

the war he had been a minor journalist; now he did editorial work. We gave him drinks at Sacher's, dinner at the Kinsky Palace, then we went on to my friend, Janet's, where there was a cosy, intimate atmosphere. As we drank our coffee, he took the floor as Russians will.

He recited Russian poetry in a clear, resonant voice. We were delighted. He then acted out whole passages of Gogol, happy, comic passages. Suddenly he broke off, sat down, took a glass of wine and announced:

'Happiness is conditional on suffering; without suffering we cannot know real happiness.' He gazed at Janet's comfortable quarters and our expensive persons. 'We crave for the new, all of us, but then we become accustomed to it and it loses its attraction.' We agreed and settled more comfortably in our chairs.

He was immersed in love poems which he recited with great feeling when he interrupted himself brusquely:

'Love isn't at all like that; it's sordid, repulsive. There's no beauty in it. We learnt that in the war. And as for war, it turns men into beasts. Better to forget it all.' He was silent for a while; then as though the words were forced out of him: 'When a man is compelled to shoot his own soldiers it turns him into a brute, a coarse brute.' There was nothing we could say; we remained silent.

After more wine and coffee he told us about his girl.

'For two years she waited for me. I was reported killed and she went to another. When I was brought home wounded she came back to me, but out of pity. I was proud, I sent her away. Was I right? Love never grows out of pity, and pity doesn't last; it turns to contempt.'

We started talking about the Austrians. 'How humiliating that they should beg for cigarettes!' he protested. 'Even well-dressed individuals. I would never beg for anything. We didn't even when there was no food. I would rather steal than beg!'

Janet's red nails attracted his attention. He was shocked by them.

'Why do you do that? It's horrible! Like blood dripping off your fingers; it's unnatural.' I translated and Janet explained that it was smart, fashionable. 'Smart! Fashionable!' he retorted. 'Such words mean nothing to me. Only the natural is beautiful!'

Talking to the Russians

Janet was laughing at him. He smiled back eagerly and with a gesture that included us all:

'How rare it is to be able to say exactly what is in one's mind!' he exclaimed. 'All over the world men must be thinking more or less the same kind of thoughts. But one's condition, one's circumstances all conspire to restrain one and I don't necessarily mean politics. It is rare to find yourself among people and in circumstances that allow you to show yourself for what you are, to say just what you think and feel.' He paused: 'Yet surely all of us are striving towards the same goals – an end to the poverty that humiliates, a little freedom and a little beauty?'

A Russian officer stopped Alec and me in the park. Did we speak Russian? He had travelled up from Hungary, he said, with some thirty questions about Britain that his group of officers would like answered. Would we do that for him? We took him to the YMCA. There over tea and cakes he brought out a scruffy piece of paper and read out the first question:

'What do you live for?'

Alec and I gazed at each other questioningly.

He explained: 'We live for the Party, for our community, for the welfare of the common man. But your morals were laid down by the Church and we gather that most Englishmen have abandoned the Church, so now what do you live for?'

Finally, I suggested that our morals were still based on Christian ethics which most people considered the best.

The next question was whether military service was compulsory before the war. 'We are not sure whether the facts we are told are always true. We want to check on them,' he said with a smile. Other questions concerned Trade Unions, Parliament, education, the army.

As soon as he reached the end of his list, he thanked us and said he must hurry back; officially he was not here at all. But my mind battled on with that first question – what did we live for?

It was Christmas. We held an 'Allied Party' in our Mess. We had a huge Christmas tree and an orchestra, Father Christmas came and there was fortune-telling; we had a crowd of people and all was festive. Into it walked a bedraggled Russian officer, his boots muddy, his uniform soiled and wet. He had come up from Hungary, he told us. It was snowing and seeing lights he wandered in hoping he might get a meal. His name was Barsoff. We fed him and invited him to join the party. When the raffle was drawn, someone arranged for Barsoff's number to be called. He marched up for his prize, undaunted by his appearance and made a speech in perfect English. Before the war, he told us, he had been secretary to the Moscow English Club. The whole room rose to applaud him.

Around midnight most people began leaving. A group of us remained congregated around Barsoff. He held us with his deep sincerity, discoursing on the world, life, death and love. He spoke of literature; he was particularly interested in Oscar Wilde and Priestley. He quoted poetry, Russian and English, to illustrate his points. It flowed from him naturally.

When Karl Heiser, my American friend, criticised the Soviet Union, Barsoff was thoughtful. Then he said:

'Yes, I agree we have made many mistakes. Much is wrong in our system. I will admit we have committed crimes; we regret them and we are ashamed. But all the same we are on the right road. Of that I am convinced, absolutely convinced.' It was four in the morning.

We saw Barsoff off and on during the next weeks and continued, Russian-style, to exchange ideas. He told us he was hoping to join the ACA. Then one night at the Opera a friend and I spotted him in the audience. We waved; he looked the other way. We tried to convey to him that we would like him to sit with us; he paid no attention. In the interval he met us as though by chance; speaking rapidly he told us that he had joined the Soviet element of the Commission as interpreter. He refused to dine with us and hurried away convinced that he had explained his behaviour.

Some of the Russian delegates especially the senior ones chatted to me during the meal breaks at ACA meetings. I never started any conversation but I valued their talk.

To Major Levitas I was an anachronism. How, before I met them, had I visualised the Soviet people? 'Was it with horns on our heads and a tail?' he wanted to know. He was not far wrong. He started talking about war and how at times it was inevitable. I interrupted to say that it was men, cruel by nature, who craved for the excitement of war; women would manage to settle disputes without fighting. But violence, he stressed, is necessary for maintaining law and order. I stated firmly that I was opposed to violence in any form and in any circumstances. 'You are straight out of Turgenev!' he cried. He did not mean it as a compliment. 'It's incredible! I would never have believed it possible in our modern times to hold such views. As for women being less cruel than men, personally I have found that when a woman is asked to investigate and report on someone, she is invariably more merciless in her indictment than a man.'

Koptelov, Chairman of the Soviet Political Division, was always eager to hold forth; he had no inhibitions about it. But then, like the generals, he was very senior. He liked to discuss religion; he specialised in different religions. Perhaps he also enjoyed teasing me or even shocking me.

'Monasteries are for lazy cowards,' he started at the beginning of a lunch break, 'for those who cannot or do not wish to face up to life.' I started protesting, but he went on: 'I know them, I lived among them.' He had grown up in Simbirsk, he told me, in Siberia, famous before the revolution for its numerous monasteries. 'Christ, if he existed,' he continued, 'went among the people to work and to preach God's truth, if it is the truth. He did not hide from life; that is the true Christian way.'

Koptelov was a slight, wiry individual, with a pale, mongolian-featured face. He wore expensive suits yet somehow managed to look scruffy. His jewelled cuff-links were out of place. Everything about him seemed to shoot up, tufts of hair, disturbed by his nervous fingers, his eyebrows, so often questioning, the tips of his collar curling upwards and the expressive gestures of his hands.

'Priests should not be exempt from work,' he announced. 'It is up to them to set an example.' The Russian priest in Vienna was paid by the Soviet authorities for one day's work a week. I knew this and wanted to protest but was too slow at thinking up answers.

Koptelov was quick to laugh. At times he could not resist making childish jokes. 'I'm going home on bus No. 11,' he announced to the other delegates, pointing to his own legs. When he came to meetings totally unprepared he took refuge in metaphors and proverbs that confused and exasperated his colleagues, but Jack Nicholls our delegate collected them in a special note-book. Koptelov concluded one conference with the words:

'Well, to sum up; man is but a sausage, whatever you stuff him with, that will he be!'

He was indignant at what he called our tolerance of the Austrian Press. 'You allow them to print photographs of Hitler! They write articles critical of the Allies!' But when faced with these same Austrians, he was considerate in his dealings with them. In his honour during lunch, the Austrian orchestra played 'Black Eyes'. He squirmed. It is a song beloved of Russian émigrés, but anathema to the Soviets. I was afraid he would make a scene, but he merely grumbled to me.

Koptelov told me about a museum which had been dedicated to my great-grandfather, Ivan Poustchine, in Siberia. It contained his books and souvenirs of the Decembrists. Many of the Russians I met knew about him and enjoyed talking about him. I had also read about him in a local Soviet newspaper.

When we somehow got onto the subject of angels, and Koptelov was capable at any moment of plunging into any subject, he grinned saying: 'The devil is more attractive. He is forceful, powerful, while the angels, they're weaklings, useless.' He resembled a jovial devil himself. And one argument he concluded with the words: 'But if Christ were alive to-day, he would be on our side, on the side of the poor, the oppressed, the workers, the proletariat.'

15

White Russians

The candlelight flickered over the Ikonastas or Golden Gates open to reveal the glittering altar crucifix; it flickered over the gold ikons, the gilded chandeliers and the jewelled crosses. In the centre of the church stood a dark cluster of old folk, White Russians who had presumably been unable to flee westward out of reach of the Red Army. There are no pews or chairs in Russian Orthodox churches; the congregation stand. Rich, emotional singing engulfed the church and in response the people made the Sign of the Cross, bowed low and fell to their knees. The priest's haggard face, thin scraggy beard and strands of grey hair falling to his shoulders, contrasted strangely with the brilliance of his vestments.

He left the splendour of the altar, came down a few steps and faced his congregation. The choir fell silent; it was time for the sermon.

The priest scanned the pale, lined faces before him, then spoke:

'Brethren! We are poor, we are hungry, but this is good for the soul.' The saints, to save their souls, had deliberately starved and lived in poverty. He gazed down kindly, his fingers caressing the golden Cross hanging on his chest. He urged his congregation to accept the difficult conditions in which they were living, to suffer their lot patiently, thus humbly sharing the fate of the Saints. 'We must submit; suffering can ennoble us all.' Suddenly, his features stern, his thin voice menacing, he cried out: 'But if any among you dare to speculate, if you should think thus to improve your lot, to increase your material comfort,' he paused; 'if any among you are speculators, you are damning your very souls!' He threatened them with heavenly wrath and severe human punishment. Finally glancing round the pitiful group before him, he opened his arms wide as though to gather them in his embrace and said gently, coaxingly: 'Bear your lot patiently. Be humble. God bless you all!'

Wherever there were White Russians abroad, their life centred around the church. The priest would know what had happened to relatives and friends of Russians in London. After the service I spoke to him. He told me most Russians had fled westward. Of those who remained, many were Austrian subjects and had little to fear. As for the others, and he gestured towards them: 'They are old, harmless. They are in my care and by now I am well known in the Soviet Commandatura – I wear them down with my requests!' He laughed. He said the congregation subsisted on bread alone and even that was scarce. He was the only Russian priest left; the others had fled. The Germans had collected together the valuables of the church, but had had no time to cart them off. On their arrival the Soviet authorities had handed the keys of the church over to him, so the church property was intact and he was able to continue the religious services. I asked after several families, but he denied any knowledge of anyone. He was friendly but firm; he did not know me and was not going to risk giving me any information.

White Russians were in a difficult position. Scattered over Europe, the young men had fought for the country in which they had settled. Members of the same family had found themselves on opposing sides. Of those who had remained stateless many had worked for the Germans, driven by an almost religious antagonism towards communism. In the eyes of the Soviets they were traitors. The priest was not giving anyone away.

Some of the congregation gathered round, attracted by my uniform. They were curious. Who was I? Where had I come from? What was I doing in Vienna? I told them and the priest stood beside me making sure nothing was said that should not be said. I noticed that no one vouchsafed any information about themselves; the priest, however, pocketed my modest contribution without hesitation.

White Russians

January 7th is the Russian Christmas. Janet came with me to the Russian church. An elderly lady, standing near me, seemed familiar. Her face was unnaturally pale, with great patches under the eyes; she was wearing a shabby black coat with a black shawl over her head. A girl of about seventeen with a round, child-like face was standing beside her, staring at me. There was a boy with them, lanky and pathetically thin. The girl nudged the woman. Then they whispered: 'Masha!'

I remembered. The woman was the wife of a White Russian parish priest we had had in London some years back. She had aged so much she was hardly recognisable. I hurried over to them. As the service was finishing we came out together. I had last heard of them before the war in Yugoslavia. Now they told me that they had worked as slave labour in Germany during the war and that the father had been killed at the front where he was chaplain to a Yugoslav regiment. I could see they had suffered, were probably hungry and possibly in danger.

We brought the mother and the girl, Kira, back to our Mess. The boy, Kiril, was feeling ill and went home. In my room I sat them down in the most comfortable chairs near the radiator. They poured out their story.

The mother began: 'You know how we feared and hated communism, so when war started and the Germans were fighting against the Communists we answered their appeal and volunteered for work in Germany. But when we arrived there, you won't believe it, but German soldiers literally rounded us up and treated us like . . . like cattle!' She fell silent, staring down at the floor, wrapping her coat more closely round her.

With a quick gesture Kira touched her mother's hand. There were tears in her eyes but she took up the story, though stifling a sob as she spoke. Meeting me was breaking down their reserve. 'Yes, they paraded us naked, the whole train-load, at a railway station with German soldiers and officers staring at us. A doctor was supposed to decide by the look of us where we should work. He lounged at a table; we had to advance slowly past him.'

Kira was staring down at the floor too. She forced herself to go on. 'It was too late to get away. We were caught. We spent the whole war as slaves, at the mercy of the people we were sent to work for, in Germany at first, then here in Austria.' Her voice faded; she was unable to go on about this German experience.

At the end of the war they landed up in the eastern part of Austria. Kira continued: 'We knew nothing of what was happening anywhere else. The Red Army streamed through the village but they didn't touch us. Kiril even gave away an extra pair of boots he had to a soldier who only had bits of leather and paper tied round his feet. But then came a regiment of NKVD troops with their Commissar officers, and the house where we were working (the owners had fled) was requisitioned for the Colonel in command.

'Mother hurriedly hung up all the ikons we possessed on the walls to protect us.' Kira was speaking more naturally now. 'The officers glanced at them but said nothing. They took over the whole house, leaving us one room. There were drunken orgies there every day; night and day Austrian women were brought in for the Colonel. But he didn't touch us; we spoke Russian and that restrained him; it made him feel ashamed. When he was drunk and became aggressive we kept well out of his way. At night, we heard screams: 'Hilfe! Hilfe!' (Help!) Austrian women came begging me to save them. I had to go out to their houses in the night. When I spoke to the soldiers in Russian, they slunk away shamefaced.'

'These Austrian women,' she was scornful, 'expected me to help them, but they hadn't helped us when we worked there as slave labour. They tried to persuade me to give myself to the Colonel so that he would leave them alone.'

The mother interrupted Kira and took up the story. 'The Colonel even invited me in for a drink,' she said. 'I told him I was old enough to be his mother. He locked the door but I kept my head and managed to get out. The next day he couldn't look me in the face.' She hesitated, then: 'But I heard one soldier say: "Age doesn't matter. Just cover the face and it's all the same."' She shuddered. 'Like animals. So horrible!' There was silence. All I could do was listen and share their anguish. She sighed and continued: 'When he got drunk again, he forced his way into our room. We had to fight him, Kiril and I, literally, but we managed to push him out and to lock the door. He banged and threatened till he fell down in a drunken stupor; he remained lying there all night in the passage. Then Kira was told that she was "needed in the Soviet Union!" '

Kira intervened: 'And the officer added that the Colonel was determined to get me. We had to escape and at once. While the Colonel was dining, we collected our things and hurried out of the house. We were standing outside, not knowing where to go when the Colonel's chauffeur appeared. He offered to drive us to the main road. There, he told us, convoys of troops were heading for Vienna and we could get a lift. He drove us in the Colonel's car.' A hint of a smile flitted over Kira's face. 'And we stopped a lorry-load of soldiers. They hauled us up and that is how we arrived here in Vienna.'

They knew nothing of the Allied zones and so remained in the Soviet zone of the city. Shortly after their arrival, everyone was obliged to register. This brought a Soviet officer with the news that Kira was wanted at the Commandatura. The Colonel, they learnt, was now also in Vienna.

The mother went on: 'I insisted on accompanying her with Kiril. We pleaded with the officer; we told him all that had happened. When we were in sight of the Commandatura, he suddenly stopped, pointed to the French zone and turned the other way. We hurried off in that direction, blessing him for his goodness and we prayed that he should not suffer for it. And so we learnt that the Allies were in Vienna and Kira now has a job with the Americans at the Allied Secretariat.'

'I still get messages from the Colonel,' Kira said, 'but the Americans protect me. The Soviets keep trying to persuade me to go to their political school in Moscow. They promise that I would be sent back to work here in Vienna and I would live here in comfort. I know girls who have done this and they are now living in a comfortable flat and they all have fur coats.' As I listened, I watched Kira's childish face and wondered at her quick smile and general air of kindliness after all she had lived through.

They were hungry. The money Kira earned was only enough to keep them supplied with potatoes. Kiril was losing his teeth. I gave her my NAAFI goods, whisky, gin, cigarettes, soap and chocolate; she could exchange them for food on the black market. I could not help feeling guilty as I handed the goods over; we were not allowed to give them away, but Kira was merely amused by my scruples.

As often as I dared, I invited them to meals in the Mess – only Allies were allowed in and this family was stateless. The mother accompanied Kira to the Mess, but refused to come to the table. She insisted on waiting in my room while we ate. Only later did Kira admit that her mother could not take her coat off as her dress had had to be sold. But Kira ate her fill and joined cheerfully in the light-hearted banter at the table. She then staggered off with a sackful of goods to sell.

I once asked Kira whether they needed anything urgently. She replied: 'My mother and I want to ask you whether you could give us a reel of black cotton.'

Mrs Kinderman, a small attractive blonde, was also White Russian. She was married to an Austrian civil servant who worked in the Ministry of Reconstruction. She was now an Austrian subject, but the Soviet authorities would know of her Russian origin. A Russian-speaking friend from our Political Division, Robin Edmunds, took me to visit them. I was curious to hear her experiences of living under the control of the Red Army.

They offered us tea, and later insisted that we share their evening meal. This was embarrassing; we knew how little they had but there was no refusing them. It was a meagre but elegantly served supper. Afterwards we talked late into the night.

I was prepared to listen to the usual Austrian-style anti-Soviet saga, but no, the Kindermans were interested in the coming elections. They told us of the lorry-loads of young people driving around Vienna, singing and waving red flags. Only the Communist Party had the use of the loudspeakers and they appeared to dominate the political scene. The Kindermans were anxious to see the Social Democrats, President Renner's party, elected. Renner, they said, was a courageous and efficient party leader.

We discussed the British Press attacks on the Russian soldiers; the Kindermans were surprised at their violence.

'It's probably a reaction against the excessive pro-Russian tendencies of British war-time propaganda,' Mr Kinderman said. 'Then every Russian was a hero. Now British journalists have come face to face with the ordinary Russian equivalent of your Smith or Jones, and they can't reconcile him with their previous vision. Time is needed for them to get things into perspective.'

I felt I could trust the Kindermans so I asked Mr Kinderman the vexed question as to whether the Soviets, when they captured the city, had or had not brought in food supplies for the city's children? The Soviets claimed they had, the Austrian authorities denied it. Mr Kinderman explained:

'From the moment of their arrival, the Russians despatched lorries to collect food for the children and continued to do so all the time during the fighting. But, as nothing is ever organised by them methodically, the food was neither weighed nor noted officially. Russians don't refuse anything for children, either officially or as individuals.'

And I asked Mrs Kinderman whether she felt the Austrians had cause to be as frightened of any Russian they met as they made out.

'I have always gone about alone and nothing has ever happened to me,' she replied. Her small regular-featured face held authority and her eyes that looked so straight at you were trusting. 'But it is only reasonable to avoid drunken soldiers whatever their nationality.' Then she answered the question I had hesitated to ask. 'The Soviet authorities have not troubled me. They treat me as an Austrian and I can sometimes help out with the language problem.'

We were impressed by this family. With the elections coming up and Mrs Kinderman being White Russian, their personal future would be most uncertain should the Communists be elected, but this had not prejudiced their views.

A young titled White Russian couple were in trouble. The husband had disappeared. My sister in America wrote asking me to help them. The wife was living in the central, jointly controlled, district of Vienna. Snow was lying on the ground but it was inside the house that the cold penetrated one's clothing. There was no heating and the thick walls kept out any sunshine. I knocked on a door and entered. The young woman was sitting up in bed, flushed with fever, her eyes

White Among the Reds

full of tears. When I told her who I was, she sobbed out her distress, unable to control herself.

'My husband went out, just for a moment and now he's disappeared. This was weeks ago, and there's no trace of him. Nothing. I don't know where he is, what's happened to him. I don't know what to do!'

An elderly woman, a Baroness I gathered when she was introduced, sat at the bedside. She was hard-featured, with thin lips and inquisitive eyes. She was dressed all in black, but it was not her clothes that made her look sinister, it was something in her manner. Baroness is a German title so I presumed she was Russian but of German origin. Was she a friend protecting or was she waiting to hear something compromising? I wanted to ask the young woman so many questions but in the presence of this other, I hesitated. The Baroness seemed to be in control here; she made no move to leave now that I had called. The young woman pleaded with me:

'Please find him, or find out what has happened. I must know.'

A girl rushed into the room, her school satchel swinging from her arm. She was rosy-cheeked, with big blue eyes and a smiling, friendly face – a small replica of what her mother must look like in her normal state. She kissed her mother and rushed out again.

'Why are you living here in the first zone?' I asked.

'It's central. I thought I might learn something here,' she explained. The Baroness never took her eyes off me. I did not dare ask anything further, and left promising to make enquiries and find out whatever I could.

I asked my friend Alec who worked in the Intelligence Corps to help. He found out that the husband had worked for the German Secret Service. He had been on the Soviet list of men wanted for committing atrocities. Alec presumed the Soviets had got him and by now he must be dead.

'Get the wife out of Vienna as fast as you can,' Alec urged.

Very reluctantly I went back again. The Baroness was sitting there as though she had never moved. Perhaps I seemed as suspicious to her as she seemed to me, but I had to speak out. I said that no one appeared to know anything about the husband but: 'You must get out of here, especially out of this central zone. You have no protection here.'

'But I can't,' the wife cried. 'He might come back here.'

'He won't. This is the last place he would come to. Much better go to your family in America. In Washington you will have influence, money, friends; they can do much more on your behalf than any of us here. I can't help you here.'

She admitted that she had the necessary papers and money which her family had sent her and arrangements had been made to fly her out through the Americans. I urged her to go and to go quickly.

'You have more chance of tracing your husband from America, and there your daughter will be safe.'

That decided her. She promised to go as soon as possible. I undertook to inform her family by telegram. The Baroness said nothing throughout.

On the eve of the Russian Easter, the greatest festival of the Orthodox Church, Olia and I went to the midnight service. The church was floodlit. Inside, as it was being repaired, we had to dive in and out of scaffolding. There was a big crowd with many Russian officers looking very smart, their wives on their arms, and there were many soldiers. They bought the biggest candles to light and place, as is the custom, before a crucifix or ikon.

The Easter Procession, headed by the priest and his acolytes in silver and white vestments, bearing religious banners, ikons and crucifixes, together with the whole congregation foregathered in front of the church. At the stroke of midnight the priest sang out triumphantly: 'Christ is Risen!' Hundreds of voices answered him: 'He is Risen indeed!' and the choir burst into song: 'Christ is Risen from the Dead!' The congregation lit their candles, the flame passing from neighbour to neighbour and illuminating their eager faces. To the festive singing the procession wound its way round and into the church, White Russian émigrés elbowing Red Army soldiers.

The Easter service was followed by the continuous joyous singing of the Easter Mass, which lasted several hours. Many stayed on for that too. There was one soldier, a middle-aged man, who stood very still, his hands in front of him round his cap, his eyes fixed on the altar crucifix, his lips mouthing the words of the service. Periodically he sighed, he made the Sign of the Cross with a wide sweep of his arm and bowed low from the waist. He knelt touching his forehead to the ground and remained there in prayer, oblivious to his surroundings – a traditional Russian peasant.

When we came out, a group of Red Army soldiers came towards us greeting us with: 'Christ is Risen!' to which the reply 'He is Risen indeed!' is customarily followed by three kisses. We hurried away as fast as was seemly. We could hear the soldiers still laughing in the distance.

16

High-Level Interpreting

'Come along to your old friend here!' Marshal Koniev, the Soviet C-in-C, exclaimed as I arrived to interpret for the first time at the Allied Council luncheon.

'That's me! Come here!' General Mark Clark, the American, called and he added: 'and now we can get rid of all these uglies!' He waved at their male interpreters who escaped with relief. A chair was placed between them and I sat down to the meal, not realising that the interpreters had stood behind their own delegate's chair and had not eaten at all. I managed to put down generous helpings of this delicious food prepared for the four C-in-Cs while interpreting for them at the same time.

I had become relief interpreter for our Colonel at Executive Committee and Allied Council meetings and I had taken over the interpreting during the lunch breaks and at conversations outside the conference room. When the Colonel left the ACA I took over the interpreting at the meetings too. He had also been Head of the Interpreters' Pool. With a new Head it was decided that I should alternate with another woman interpreter recently arrived in Vienna. Our new chief had no experience of interpreting. He saw no need for continuity or for interpreters at high-level meetings to prepare for them or to be briefed. Yet any subject, however specialised, might crop up and delegates often plunged straight into an argument started at a previous meeting. Without seeing the agenda the interpreter would not even know what was being discussed.

Without saying anything I had made my own arrangements with the generals' ADCs. Before each meeting I went down to their office and studied the agenda and the General's briefs, and I looked up subjects I did not understand and words I did not know.

Also a Soviet interpreter had asked me as 'Mother of the Interpreters' to correct any mistakes they made. We had discussed it and had agreed to make a sign whenever one of us made a mistake thus giving us a chance to correct it; it relieved some of the tension.

On the alternate meeting of the Executive Committee my colleague, as had been arranged, appeared as interpreter; she had not been briefed and was unprepared. She was unable to grasp what the delegates were discussing and floundered helplessly through the translation. She was asked not to come again and, humiliated, gave up the job. I carried on alone coping in my own way.

Our Admin. let us down even over such a simple matter as providing transport. We constantly had to cadge lifts when it failed to appear. At one Executive Committee meeting, taking my presence for granted, General Winterton, our Deputy C-in-C, made a speech and was wondering why it was followed by silence. At that moment I turned up. Fortunately he merely laughed.

I was overawed at my first meeting of the Allied Council. It was under Russian Presidency. The International Secretariat flew the four Allied flags with a Russian Guard of Honour drawn up in front, the officers wearing white gloves and ceremonial swords. The band greeted each Commander-in-Chief on arrival; he then inspected the Guard of Honour, the officers baring their swords as they reported. Inside Soviet soldiers guarded the conference rooms, standing at attention.

Meetings were held in a vast hall with a big square table in the centre. Each C-in-C sat in the middle of his side of the table, his Deputy on his one side, his Political Adviser on the other. Behind him sat the two interpreters, Russian and French or English. The secretaries and experts were grouped at the back, some sixty persons in all. The first time I stood up to translate, Marshal Koniev who was in the chair smiled and nodded to me.

High-Level Interpreting

During their Presidency in the Allied Council, the Russians beat the record for short meetings, all of them lasting less than two hours. The French beat the record in the opposite direction, one of their meetings lasting for fifteen hours.

It was difficult to summon up the correct words at such drawn-out meetings. When, after hours of disagreement General McCreery, our C-in-C, and Marshal Koniev were locked in angry dispute, glaring at each other, accusing each other of inaccuracy or even dishonesty, sitting behind him, I could see McCreery's neck flush a bright red and I knew he was about to lose his temper. On one occasion, he called Koniev a rude word. My rude vocabulary being limited in any language, I searched hurriedly for a suitable Russian equivalent; nothing came to mind. Koniev stared up at me, ready for the insult. All I could blurt out was: 'You are very . . . bad!' The Marshal's hand went swiftly up to cover his face and he stared down at the table. There was silence. Then as Chairman he announced that they had gone far enough in disagreement and he deemed it wiser to close the meeting. I ran into him later in the corridor.

'So I am bad, am I?' he mocked me. I hurried past, muttering that I was too tired to be able to think.

General Winterton once said: 'Let's stop being like a blushing spinster and come out into the open.' Exhausted, I left out the 'blushing spinster'. Winterton was on to it at once.

'I bet you didn't translate that!' he exclaimed, turning round to face me. I had to admit that I had not. The whole room laughed as the joke was translated for the Russian and French delegates.

Winterton was most refreshing to work for. Exhausted and irritated, he still retained a sense of humour. Whenever the Russians wished to demonstrate extreme displeasure, they marched demonstratively out of the conference room. This happened whenever subjects were discussed against their wishes. General Zheltov had once gone straight upstairs to play ping-pong. The next time Zheltov rose dramatically to his feet and strode out at the head of his following, Winterton wagged a finger playfully:

'But no ping-pong, Alexis! No ping-pong!'

On another occasion the Russian delegate complained that an Austrian singer, a known Nazi, was appearing on the stage in the American zone. The American delegate protested that she was a woman and a great artist, but he finally agreed to make enquiries into her past activities. At the next meeting, he reported that his people were prepared to remove the singer from the stage.

'But she ranks as a first class singer; she is spreading culture!' the Russian protested. 'Artists stand above politics!' As they all gazed at him in amazement, the Frenchman announced:

'I disagree. A Nazi should not be allowed to perform in public however great an artist he or she may be.' General Winterton suggested they should all once again look into the matter and come to a final decision at the next meeting. A week later, Winterton proposed that the artist should be banned from the stage in all the Allied zones. The Frenchman was irate:

'That's ridiculous! Each case must be judged on its merits. This particular case should be treated with sympathy. A young woman, beautiful, surrounded by temptation.'

Winterton interrupted: 'Now look here! What's going on? And why have I been left out?' The others looked embarrassed. Winterton laughed and was magnanimous enough to drop the subject.

On another occasion Winterton suspected General Zheltov of misquoting an Austrian law in order to bolster up his own argument, but our legal section were unable to trace this law. He turned to me:

'Find out what law he is quoting.' I went across the room and asked one of the Russian secretaries to find it out for me. He returned with a slip of paper quoting the law we were seeking. Sure enough Zheltov was misquoting. Winterton was triumphant. He leant forward and at that moment I realised what I had done. Urgently I pulled at Winterton's sleeve and explained.

He turned to Zheltov: 'Our apologies; I was about to blast you with ammunition most generously supplied by your own side. I will say no more.' I was very grateful.

All were agreed that the Russian Presidency had gone very well but, the responsibility for security also falling on the Russians, we had failed to foresee what this entailed. During lunch Winterton asked me to fetch out of his brief-case in the conference room a document which was highly confidential and directed against the Soviets. Two Russian sentries stood outside. I explained what I

High-Level Interpreting

wanted and they let me pass. I opened the door. There were two more sentries inside, but there were also two Russians in civilian clothes who had no business there and who, as I entered, drew rapidly away from the conference table. The General's brief-case lay there – 'guarded' by Russians! I picked it up and hurried upstairs. Winterton was considerably shaken.

General Winterton was equally pleasant to work for on social occasions. The Russians were celebrating Red Army Day (February 23rd) and I accompanied him to the dinner. Marshal Koniev was our host. Presiding in the middle of a long table, he radiated a friendly relaxed atmosphere that embraced everyone present. I sat opposite Winterton who was next to an extremely distinguished-looking Russian general with the frankest smile and a rich speaking voice, whom we had not seen before. He looked bronzed and healthy. He was Colonel-General Kurasov, Koniev's Deputy Commander of the Third Ukrainian Front. He spoke of himself as 'an old man' at forty-nine, the same age as Koniev. Winterton immediately fell into conversation with him, bubbling over as usual with humour and vivacity. When he left the table to greet a colleague, Kurasov leant over towards me and wanted to know who this 'charmer' was and all about him.

He then exclaimed: 'It is extraordinary! We meet for the first time and we are talking like old friends!'

He told us this was the Red Army's twenty-eighth birthday. With pride he showed us his medal for twenty years' service. Winterton remarked pointedly:

'The Red Army is probably the best Russia has ever had. Still, it is not the only army.' Kurasov laughed and exclaimed:

'Of course not!'

Looking at the priest, who was also present, he described how when they had entered Vienna and the priest had seen Soviet officers wearing epaulettes, he had made the Sign of the Cross and cried out:

'Thank God! All is as it was!' To demonstrate, Kurasov made an exaggerated Sign of the Cross and laughed heartily.

Beside me sat a silent lady of vast proportions who turned out to be Kurasov's wife. She was wearing a black décolleté dress. Suddenly a strap gave and she was obliged to hold the dress up with her hand. She sat there embarrassed and helpless. I whispered to her that we should leave the table together. I helped her up and we searched and found a ladies' room where a maid sewed the strap on again. The lady never uttered a word, but when we got back to our places we sat in a companionable silence and Winterton smiled encouragingly at her.

He was not eating much. A Russian maid was about to serve him a second helping when he waved his hand in refusal. But she insisted.

'You must eat more; you are much too skinny. This is good wholesome food.' He turned round in surprise to look up at the girl. She smiled unconcernedly and passed on to his neighbour.

Winterton started darting around the table greeting people and exchanging jokes. After dinner there was dancing. Most of the Russian wives were voluminous. Winterton swept them off their feet one after another. I came across him with an enormous lady in his arms. Afterwards he told us she was wonderful, full of determination and she just bore him along. And he added: 'She was mighty!'

We hopped and galloped through traditional Russian dances, the Krakoviak and the Grand Rond, General Zheltov in the lead, rushing us off our feet as we all held hands in a large circle. Winterton's laugh resounded above the music of the balalaika and concertina band whenever he made mistakes and collided with others. He caught General Mark Clark by the hand and pressed him into the circle too.

When we reverted to ordinary ballroom dancing, General Clark complained to me that all the other girls were so small, but he added that it was all good fun. General Lebedenko, the Soviet Commandant, invited me to a waltz. His stomach protruded so far that I was balanced on its tip as he swung me round expertly, puffing away into my ear. He was amazingly light on his feet.

Young privates whirled around on the floor under our feet, doing the Russian dance. General Clark wound his way carefully and without comment round them. Winterton slapped them on the back, admired their acrobatics, and encouraged them to greater feats. He was fascinated by their complete unselfconsciousness, prancing in and out of the legs of all the generals. He kept repeating to everyone what fun it all was.

We were very late coming back. Winterton remarked: 'Well, I enjoyed every moment and without drink too; that was good, as I have been forbidden drink. And how nice they all are – and yet, on

Monday we shall begin quarrelling all over again. Why is it, they will be so impossible?' I had asked General Clark whether he liked the Russians better, now that he had seen them in a relaxed atmosphere. He answered: 'Yes, socially, but only socially.'

In the Allied Council General Kurasov began to replace Marshal Koniev who was supposed to be on leave. He presided courteously and with dignity, unruffled by the constant rudeness shown him by both General Clark and General McCreery. He may have thought it their natural manner, since he was continually subjected to it even over minor matters. But he was no diplomat.

General Kurasov was standing in a doorway with two Austrian officials as I was passing along the corridor in the International Secretariat. He beckoned to me and asked me to help him as his German was not very good. They were discussing a loan which the Russians were proposing to make to the Austrians. When it was over they thanked me and I thought no more about it. The next day our delegate interrupted a meeting of the Allied Council to accuse General Kurasov of having one-sided discussions with the Austrians concerning a loan. Without hesitation, Kurasov disclaimed all knowledge of any such discussions. As he spoke he stared straight ahead and that happened to be straight at me. There was no time to think; my decision had to be immediate. Rightly or wrongly I said nothing.

Very soon Kurasov began to lose that good-humoured serenity that distinguished him when we first saw him. He became pale and looked care-worn. He kept repeating that he wished he was back with the army.

When he was looking particularly harassed and worried, Winterton asked whether anything was wrong. Kurasov told us that he had just learnt that his son in Hungary had recently had a motor-cycle accident and had been several months in hospital. Later, meeting Zheltov, Winterton asked him how the boy was. Zheltov knew nothing about it. In trouble affecting him so personally, Kurasov had confided in Winterton rather than in Zheltov, his Political Commissar. I had noticed that Russians kept their personal and family affairs very much to themselves. The less known, the safer. I should have remembered this and warned Winterton. Kurasov had trusted him and we had let him down.

17

The Iron Curtain

Clashes at meetings between East and West so often occurred because neither side knew the circumstances that prompted the other's point of view. Each side took it for granted that the other was thinking along the same lines, which they were not. Was London aware of this?

Alec, whom I consulted, suggested I write a report and he would forward it to his Intelligence people in London. I did this.

In my report I stressed the differences between the Russian attitude towards the conquered nations and our own. We wished to build up prosperous countries; the Russians were determined to take everything but the bare minimum for their survival from the conquered nations, in order to feed their own hungry population and to rebuild their war-shattered country.

They were deeply hurt by our apparent indifference to the suffering of their countrymen. They did not realise how difficult it was for Westerners to imagine the devastation caused by two armies, German and Soviet, fighting twice over the whole territory of Russia proper, nor the terrible consequences for the Russian people.

They were shocked by our public condemnation of the brutal behaviour of the Red Army which, to them, was an inevitable outcome of the kind of savage war they had been forced to fight. Soviet soldiers had no Red Cross to take care of them, no relief from the war and army life except drink. Their war had been so abominable that I rarely heard a soldier or officer reminisce about it; all wished to wipe it from their memories as quickly as possible. Lieut-Col. Miasnikov of the Internal Affairs Division said that until they met up with us, they had had no idea how low they had sunk. Even now, almost a year since the war ended, Russian soldiers had no means of finding out whether their families were alive or dead.

Russian suspicion of our Western world went very deep. The great Stalin himself had been hood-winked by the Germans, and many Russians, unhappy under their own regime, had been lured over by the Germans into betraying their own country only to be treated by them with utter contempt. Russians, accustomed to thinking of the Western world as one unit, tended to associate the whole Western 'Capitalist' world with this German treachery. Russian traditional suspicion of all foreigners had hardened.

Conquest for the Russians meant aggrandisement. They presumed that their retreat from land they had conquered in Austria was carried out by arrangement with us over the division of spoils. They held old-fashioned ideas; what I conquer is mine, or at least to be used for my benefit. Most Russians could not believe, for instance, that France was free to choose her own form of government without regard to our wishes.

As I quoted verbatim from conversations with Russians, I made Alec promise that the report would be kept secret. He sent it to London. When I arrived there myself, to visit my mother who had fallen ill, I was asked to come for an interview to the War Office. There I was encouraged to elaborate. Other members of the ACA working in other spheres, who were also worried, had promised to send in reports at the same time to their own head offices in London. We were not claiming to know the rights and wrongs of these attitudes; we merely wished to point out that the two sides were drifting dangerously apart, becoming enemy camps partly as a result of avoidable misunderstandings.

On my return to Vienna members of the ACA began telling me they found my report interesting and helpful. It was good that the information had been passed on but I had not expected the report itself to be sent here. I did not want it to get back to the Russians. I did not want them to connect me in any way with any kind of

The Iron Curtain

intelligence work or spying. I had refused a request from our Air Division Intelligence section to supply them with information about Russian Air Force personnel; as an interpreter I was not required to do anything of that kind. But now one afternoon I found a Russian officer standing alone in the office of our Head of the Interpreters' Pool. I escorted him out, then returned and tried the drawer of the desk. It was unlocked. Inside lay an army journal with my report printed in it. It was marked 'Secret' but that was no consolation.

An American Intelligence officer told me he had read the report. General Winterton, our Deputy C-in-C, demanded to see a copy. Soon everyone in Vienna must have read it. Alec told me that it was appearing in memoranda to British officials and forces in other capitals abroad including Moscow and finally that Ernest Bevin, then Foreign Minister, was given a copy to read before undertaking his trip to the Soviet Union. Though there was nothing sensational in it, the report had become an important document. Was it possible that our people were so ignorant of Russian feelings?

The report set us all to thinking about East and West attitudes. We discussed them in the Interpreters' Pool with the British military and we even managed to get some Russian views. Nicholas Raevsky, a White Russian, now interpreting for the French insisted that:

'The hope of the world lies in our eastern ideal.' He was a quiet man with dark expressive eyes in a still pale face. He spoke almost reverently. 'Hope lies in our Russian attitude to life, a religious attitude, an attitude that concerns itself primarily with the soul, a Dostoevsky-like attitude. That is the true Russian way.' Raevsky was an officer in the French Foreign Legion. He was involved in the repatriation of French prisoners of war from the Soviet Union. He told us he held long conversations with Soviet officers as they sat over their drinks late into the night. He said some NKVD (KGB) officers, tormented by feelings of guilt and haunted by terror of the Devil, drank themselves into oblivion. 'Don't think that the Soviets are Godless; they know and fear God. Hence the fierceness of their anti-religious campaigns. Russia will come through in the end; she will point the way of truth to the rest of the world.'

Ishkoff, another interpreter, also White Russian, was sipping the wine Raevsky brought us from his French canteen. He interrupted him impatiently: 'I'm for the American ideal, the ideal of progress. What you're saying is old-fashioned nonsense. I don't want your soul-searching world. I prefer to own a car!' They were voicing the traditional division among Russian intellectuals, the so-called Slavophiles and Westerners.

Two Soviet officers in giving us their opinion of our Western way of life revealed their own attitude. 'You English, you only work so as to be able to arrange comfortable lives for yourselves,' one of them said. 'You do not care about the work itself, nor do you work for the common good; the welfare of humanity does not interest you. Nor do you devote yourselves wholeheartedly to any ideal.'

The other added: 'I would find it boring just living for myself, for my own amusement, without aim, or benefit to anyone else and to spend time in activities that had neither educational nor cultural value.'

Sam Beasley, an army friend, attacked me. 'You are as bad as the Soviets. You keep wanting to give yourself wholeheartedly to some cause, to some guiding principle, some ideal. It's unnatural; one can't live on such a high plane. And you exaggerate the whole time. Why not take the happy medium? Relax! Stick to reasonable principles, without fanaticism. Just enjoy life!'

And Colonel Gordon-Smith, our Deputy Commandant, explained the Englishman's suspicion of ideals. 'Englishmen have no ideals,' he stated. 'They don't know themselves what their aims are. They never wage war for something, always against something. They see clearly what they wish to avoid. Just trace history from the days of Magna Carta to our times; you'll see, our laws, our institutions have developed out of consideration for what people do not want.'

'Isn't that rather negative?' I suggested.

'On the contrary. It is better so. It isn't easy to decide what is right, what is good, whereas evil can be recognised by everyone.'

Russians have always been 'talkers', the Soviets were 'workers' as well. When we invited the Russian ADCs to play tennis or to go out with us in the evening, they invariably refused. When we insisted, one said:

'There is so little time and so much to do, to learn. Every evening I study but I need so much more time; I am so ignorant.' And at a meeting when we apologised for yawning after a late night, the Russian delegate told us that he worked regularly till two or three in the morning and got up without difficulty every day at seven.

Were the Russians so fanatically keen because education, art, literature were newly available and exciting whereas we already took them for granted? Was modern Russia succeeding in welding together the two age-old rival philosophies, that of the Slavophiles and the Westerners, the messianic and the materialistic?

Sam Beasley put his finger on another important difference between East and West when he said: 'Compromise. That's what life is about. You don't know how to compromise.' I resented his addressing this to me, but it was true of Russians in general. For them compromise was unacceptable. There was only one right, one correct way of living, one aim towards which all should strive. They did not accept that there might be several equally good ways of doing things and that a compromise might represent the best for all concerned. The Russian Orthodox Church had formerly taught the one truth; the Soviets continued this tradition.

During a conference I pointed out to a Russian delegate that he had agreed to a compromise being accepted as the best solution to a problem the meeting had discussed. How did he feel about compromise now? He was surprised and became thoughtful.

While we argued on, we were convinced that in Vienna something positive had been achieved. It was the only place in the world where the four Allies mixed freely and without serious trouble. In Berlin East and West kept to their zones. The four Allies were governing the country together in spite of all the differences and clashes and they were working towards some vague idea of general peace and reconciliation.

Now suddenly in the United Nations Bevin and Vyshinsky, the two Foreign Ministers, attacked each other bitterly. Tension gripped the whole ACA and spread rapidly throughout the country.

The Russians became silent, withdrawn. At a dinner I mentioned Bevin and Vyshinsky to Miasnikov. He listened but said nothing. Then a few days later a Soviet delegate suddenly started talking about the UN and he laughed, reminding us that Bevin and Vyshinsky, after their quarrel, came out of the meeting arm-in-arm and later were seen drinking together. So the Russians had been ordered to make light of the affair. Perhaps things were not so bad, after all.

Then came the bomb-shell – Churchill's speech at Fulton launching the 'Iron Curtain'. The word 'war' burst into our midst. We were stunned. Was this to be the end of our friendships, our hopes, our achievements? It was incredible, cruel.

Meetings continued. We avoided each others' eyes. We spoke strictly of local affairs. There was silence even among ourselves.

Ilichev, of the Internal Affairs Division, was the first to break out. At the end of a meeting he rose to go, then suddenly turned back and almost shouted: 'Who wants war when everyone is hungry and territories are devastated? It is all such a disappointment to us, such a very great disappointment. To use the word 'war' and in connection with our two countries!'

I did not know what to say. 'But Churchill is not Prime Minister.'

'It makes no difference.' Ilichev was impatient. 'He is the great war hero. He is the great statesman, making an important public speech. What he says counts.' He stood lost in thought, then went on: 'One can quarrel, we can abuse each other – all that we expected – but to introduce the word 'war'? What on earth should we fight each other for? Is anything that important?' He marched out of the room followed by a grave-faced deputy.

All was indecision, as though we were waiting, expecting something. I discussed my fears with Alan, our Consul. He showed me his comments in a letter to his parents. 'I am not at all sure that the deterioration of relations so quickly is not a good thing, since it at least gives us a chance to put things right again before everybody has forgotten what war is like, and may be a means to creating some sort of modus vivendi which could lead to a lasting peace; but it is slow work, if it can be called work at all, since no one seems to be doing much about it actively here.'

A few weeks later Ilichev came in smiling again. 'We don't have to quarrel any more in the Allied Council,' he announced. 'The crisis has passed. All is well.' And he took his place calmly at the meeting, looking round cheerfully. He was like a barometer, one moment

The Iron Curtain

plunging us into gloom and the next raising our spirits. But he had not explained his cheerfulness and the fear remained with us.

The Austrians were under considerable strain. We visited our friends the Kindermans. They were wondering whether their country was about to become the next battleground. 'Is it possible that you would go to war?' they asked. They told us that many Austrians were actually hoping for war, hoping that Russia would be destroyed by the Allies without considering what this would entail. We tried to reassure them. Robin Edmunds of our Political Division who had taken me there pointed out that the UN was the scene of so much political intrigue that speeches should not be taken seriously. But some members of the British community were already making enquiries as to how they would be repatriated before fighting started.

I accompanied General Winterton on a visit to his Soviet opposite number, General Zheltov. Ostensibly it was to get permission for the Allies to use those parts of the Wiener Wald that were in the Soviet zone. In fact Winterton wanted to find out the exact state of our relations with the Russians. Zheltov rose to greet us in the friendliest manner and agreed immediately to Winterton's request. 'Of course they can use the Wiener Wald; obviously it's for everyone to enjoy.' He beamed enthusiastically. When we got back Winterton insisted that I should remember the exact words used by Zheltov. It was important to gauge the exact amount of friendliness shown. It was all very bewildering and very troubling.

Our own little world was badly shaken; the Iron Curtain was down and international events overshadowed our relations with the Russians. The strain was great, but the work had to go on and we became accustomed to the constant background tension.

A Soviet sentry in the International Secretariat was complaining about having to take care of the French delegates. 'They are not real Allies. They didn't fight the Germans. They caved in and now they throw their weight around and I am expected to hang their coats up for them!' I asked him: 'But if it came to war between us Allies, would you fight against us?'

He hesitated, then said: 'If Stalin gives the order, yes.'

18

Spring Feeling

Sunshine flooded my room. I flung open my windows which faced the park and leaned out. The trees were bursting into leaf in vivid splashes of green; there were snowdrops, violets and primroses in the garden below. The sun was hot on my arms and face. It was Sunday. Janet and I hurried out. In the park the town's citizens were basking in the warmth. Girls hung on to soldiers' arms and couples disappeared behind the thickening hedges. No one was taking non-fraternisation seriously. In the Interpreters' Mess we filled vases with flowers and leafy branches and we sun-bathed on my balcony.

This spring-feeling enveloped us all, even the delegates at meetings. When I removed my jacket the Russian General asked how much more was I proposing to take off? General Winterton intervened with: 'It's all right. She's only doing a strip-tease act!'

On April Fool's Day, camouflaging my voice, I phoned Alec in the Intelligence section informing him that Colonel Gordon-Smith, our Deputy Commandant, required his help with an Allied parade that afternoon and he was to phone him immediately. Later I received a call back from the Colonel furious at being disturbed by such childishness. I was hurt, but it was only Alec getting his own back! I phoned Mr Cole, acting head of our Police and told him that his Russian counterpart was on his way to consult him. Mr Cole interrupted a conference, cleared the decks of confidential material and

Spring Feeling

sat waiting a whole hour. When I phoned and asked his secretary to tell him he was an April Fool she replied: 'Tell him yourself!'

The RAF's birthday is also on April 1st. I received an invitation to the RAF ball and Alan, our Consul, who was also going, invited me to dine with him first. I asked one of our French interpreters to telephone Alan for me, to inform him that at the ball he was expected to partner the Russian Consul's wife and to make a short speech. Alan became very agitated; he refused at first, then hesitated and finally to my dismay, since he was supposed to be partnering me, agreed to do so. Over dinner Alan was silent, then he told me what he had agreed to do. I was very annoyed; only as we were leaving, did I tell him he was an April Fool and it took some time to convince him that this really was so.

The Allies were present in force in the Schönbrunn Palace where the RAF ball was held. In between dances I helped the Russians out, but as soon as the music started up they waved me back to my partner.

General Morozov, their Chief of Staff, marched in. I hurried over and whispered to him that his jacket was torn at the back. He immediately placed himself back to the wall and stood their nonchalantly smoking cigarette after cigarette. When I told him he was an April Fool, he said I was as silly as his wife; she had phoned him pretending to be a young girl, wanting a date. It was all most refreshing after the weeks of strain.

British newspapers at home now talked of 'fundamental' differences between the Russians and ourselves, but with the spring feeling in the air and all things seeming possible we felt optimistic and continued our efforts to bring the two sides together.

British journalists in Vienna had been trying to persuade me to bring Russians to their Public Relations Mess as they never had occasion to meet them socially. I had been reluctant to do so only because I was afraid they might embarrass their guests. Our people were unable to meet Russians without pestering them about politics, though most Russians knew even less about politics than the average person at home. I was also afraid that what was said in private might

White Among the Reds

be quoted by the Press. But now with relations so strained I readily agreed to bring three Russian guests and we would see how things went. I was promised there would be no political discussions; the evening would be devoted entirely to pleasure.

We were served an excellent dinner with plenty to drink but not enough to confuse the mind. Colonel Gordon-Smith and Popski were among the guests as well as Michael Burn, the new *Times* correspondent. The three Russians, two officers and a girl, were made to feel at home and they relaxed. They ate their fill, drank, sang and danced. Their very real enjoyment was infectious and soon the whole Mess was drawn in around them. One of them had a fine singing voice. Requests were flung at him and he filled the room with rich, passionate singing and then with tender, nostalgic longing. The journalists surrounded him, hugging him, slapping him on the back and telling him what a 'wonderful' fellow he was and how they had never met Russians like him before.

When the Russians began saying good-bye, the girl, her yellow curls flying, her blue eyes mischievous, her smile enticing, was hemmed in by a crowd of newsmen. She refused to leave. One of her companions reminded her that she must behave or she would again be sent to a 'correction camp'.

She laughed back: 'It's all worth it a thousand times.'

I promised to come again the next Friday night when the journalists would themselves invite a few Russians.

Six Russians appeared all from the Commandatura. Colonel Nigel Dugdale, the President of the Public Relations Mess, headed the table with the senior Russian officer (officially referred to as Head of Mission) and myself on either side. The meal was as animated as the previous time; again there was no heavy drinking. It was the eve of the anniversary of the capture of Vienna by the Russians so Nigel spoke a few words of congratulation to the Red Army.

A young Russian officer jumped to his feet: 'Let us drink to our friendship. May it last for ever!'

Another sprang up proposing: 'The Allies without whom the Red Army would not have been able to achieve all it did!' The company was pleased; the toasts were spontaneous and rang out sincerely.

There was dancing. The Russians were persuaded to do their own

Spring Feeling

dances. I was whirled off my feet in the Vingerka, Krakoviak and the Russian dance. The others encircled us clapping out the rhythm and humming the tunes, which they picked up from the Russians.

I became a regular guest at the Public Relations Mess Friday parties, which became Red Army nights.

Michael Burn, the new *Times* correspondent in Vienna, always tried to be scrupulously fair in his reports and was always able to see the other side's point of view. I had met Michael on several occasions and now we often got together to discuss Russian problems. Michael was handsome, had the MC and knew he looked good. In his green jacket and black trousers he fitted perfectly into the glittering setting of the Kinsky Palace. Our generals liked and trusted him and I found him a willing and open-minded listener. I said to Michael that there was so much I wanted to explain to people at home about the Russians, but there was so little opportunity to do so. He answered: 'Why not do it through me? I am a journalist.' It was true; he could help and he did through his articles in *The Times*. A number of them he submitted to Russian journalists for their comment and if he found their criticism fair, he changed his text.

In an article on 'What the Russians think about the British' he had written: 'A good deal of their information is out of date.' The Russian comment was: 'True. As well as British information on Russia.' And on his comment that the Russians 'say with regret that America and Russia are two huge and uncouth forces which are bound, in some way or another, to clash and the accomplished, but rather soft British, will be squashed between them,' their comment was 'Nonsense!' In an article about 'What the British think about the Russians', Michael commented on the lack of individual initiative in the Russians stating that they 'are afraid of making a mistake because of the penalties.' The Russian comment was: 'True about non-intelligent people all over the world as well as Russians.'

In Vienna we had two spring parades in which, in spite of the

C-in-Cs inspecting troops.

Russian Band in uniforms designed by Gen. Winterton.

Soviet troops marching past the C-in-Cs.

French Chasseurs Alpins marching past C-in-Cs.

White Among the Reds

angry exchanges between the leaders of East and West, the four Allies put on a fine show together.

Nigel Dugdale invited me to join the Press for the 'Liberation of Vienna' Parade. He wanted me to arrange for all the newsmen to be admitted though they had only been issued with eleven passes. At the check point I told the journalists to file past quickly, while I handed the tickets to the Russian sentry and he counted them. He protested that there were more men than tickets and that orders were orders and they could not pass. I kept arguing till everyone was through and I was the only one left. I slipped past him saying: 'Well, goodbye!' He shrugged his shoulders, grinning good-humouredly. We all settled down on the window-sill in a building facing the tribune.

I had marched with members of the Allied Executive Committee all over the Schwarzenberg Platz as they planned this parade. General Zheltov, the Russian Deputy C-in-C, insisted on his own choice of where the four C-in-Cs should meet the Parade Commander. He chose the middle of the square immediately below a WC notice. The others tried to dissuade him but he remained obdurate. I was asked to explain the letters to him; Zheltov was not amused. Then it was decided that the C-in-Cs after inspecting the troops were to march across the parade ground back to the tribune to the music of the band of the Chasseurs Alpins. These march at double speed, so the C-in-Cs would be scurrying across the parade ground. It took several rehearsals to iron out all such problems.

The Russians were presiding at the time, so the Commander of the Parade was a Russian, General Komarov. The C-in-Cs marched together towards the General who, eyes forward, sword drawn, was goose-stepping towards them. Two photographers dashed forward one kneeling right in front of the General. He ignored him and marched straight on, his outstretched sword just missing the photographer's ear as the man flung himself sideways. The photographers then kept their distance. To our astonishment the Russians came out smartest, especially their band in blue trousers with red-fronted jackets and white gloves (a uniform suggested by General Winterton). Our troops were in ill-fitting battledress and heavy black boots. Our band was the smallest and General McCreery, our C-in-C, was absent,

Spring Feeling

General Winterton taking his place. But it was heartening to watch the Allies and the Austrian government laying wreaths together at the foot of the Soviet War Memorial and to see General Mark Clark standing close to Marshal Koniev, the Soviet C-in-C, and both of them chatting amiably.

No Russian troops took part in the Allied Victory Parade in London. When I told Koptelov, the Head of their Political Division, how disappointed we all were and particularly the British public, he replied that their Military Attaché was there to represent the country and that it was too complicated to transport troops. Then he quickly changed the subject. The Russians had not dared expose their soldiers to the kind of criticism that had been appearing in our Press, but they had badly misjudged the feelings of the British public who, we felt, would have given them a grand welcome.

In Vienna we had a fine Victory Parade. The sun shone, the mood was festive. Austrians crowded the pavements and cheered together with all of us Allies. Mr Cole, of our Police Division, presented me with a bouquet of roses, the first of the season, which we pinned to our uniforms. The Russians were as smart as ever but we also put on an impressive show with a detachment of Argyle and Sutherland Highlanders who were very picturesque, highly disciplined and swung arrogantly along to the music of the pipes. All the troops paraded with confidence and were cheered and applauded. It was a good and most satisfying show.

Kilts were new to the Russians and Austrians. They provoked silly jokes. That night there were numerous fights. The slighest smirk from a Russian and up came the Scotmen's fists. The Russians were impressed since the Scots, unlike themselves, were unarmed. The jokes ceased and crowds collected to watch the Argyle and Sutherland Highlanders changing guard outside Schönbrunn Palace.

We celebrated at Colonel Gordon-Smith's. I had come late, straight from a conference and found Alan dancing with a most attractive Polish lady; he had not waited for my arrival. Jealous, I started flirting with a Dutch general. We were all in a festive, light-hearted mood. The Dutch general and I began doing fancy ballet dancing consisting mostly of great leaps in the air. He was a heavy man and I was no light-weight. The others laughed so much they stopped

Troops marching from Red Army War Memorial.

Gen. Lebedenko, Marshal Koniev, Gen. Mark Clark, Gen. Winterton, Chancellor Figl and Herr Gruber before the Memorial.

Spring Feeling

dancing to watch us and Alan left his partner. The commander of the Argyle and Sutherland Highlanders, Colonel Malcolm, sat silent all evening drinking by himself. Around midnight he jumped up and launched into sword dances and gave a realistic imitation of a bagpipe player. Then, as suddenly, he took his leave formally and departed.

We had a final drink to 'Victory'. We felt reassured by the festive atmosphere of our Victory Parade. The Iron Curtain was not impenetrable.

19

Change of Commanders-in-Chief

Two top command changes followed each other in quick succession. It was officially announced that General McCreery, our C-in-C, was to be transferred to Germany. After a meeting of the Allied Council Marshal Koniev led me over to McCreery. He wished to give a farewell dinner in his honour at his Residence in the Soviet zone. He also invited General Winterton, our Deputy C-in-C, and Mr Mack, our Political Adviser. Turning to me he added: 'And I would like to invite you too.' McCreery was pleased and accepted on behalf of all of us.

The day of the dinner our office as usual was most unhelpful. The Head of the Interpreters' Pool expressed surprise when I asked for permission to leave the office early in order to change and be ready on time. Two officers were accompanying McCreery as interpreters, he said, and women were not wanted. I told him that Marshal Koniev had invited me personally. He murmured: 'Nonsense,' and refused to listen further.

As I left the office after work, I passed McCreery's car outside the Schönbrunn Palace. Then McCreery himself appeared. He called out to me to be ready on time; I would be picked up at the Palace. I told him that two officers had been allocated to him as interpreters.

'I know nothing about them.' He spoke curtly. 'But you are invited, so hurry up and dress.' I ran.

We travelled in a cavalcade. An armoured car full of Soviet

Change of Commanders-in-Chief

machine-gunners, sporting a large Soviet flag in front on one side and a large Union Jack on the other, drove ahead, followed by the escorting officer's car; then General McCreery's two-seater open sports car in which he drove alone, followed by General Winterton and myself; the last car carried Mr Mack with the ADCs and the two interpreters and another load of machine-gunners with flags flying brought up the rear. We sped through Vienna, sirens blaring, across the Danube, into the Soviet zone of Vienna, and so into the country. The populace scattered before us automatically, without looking round.

Ahead, a herd of cows approached the road. As the first armoured car passed, a cow stepped onto the road right in front of McCreery's car. He braked and stopped. The whole herd clambered onto the road; one cow sniffed at McCreery's head. The machine-gunners sprang out of their armoured car, shouting and waving their machine-guns. The cows moo-ed and mouched around. Our whole cavalcade had come to a stop. Winterton grinned as he leant forward to get a better view. McCreery had disappeared among the cows. Finally a cow stepped off the road and the rest followed, the cowherd sauntering after them.

Marshal Koniev's Residence gave nothing away about his personal taste or private life. It was just a stately mansion with minimal furniture, bare of any personal ornament or possession. On the walls hung only two portraits, one of Lenin, the other of Stalin. The Marshal greeted us at the door. He hoped we had had a pleasant journey and turned to the escorting officer who reported on the incident of the cows.

'Who was driving them, our people or the Austrians?' Koniev asked quietly.

'An Austrian,' was the reassuring answer.

We were ushered into the reception room. The ADCs and interpreters disappeared upstairs, where we later learnt they were presented with an orgy of food and drink and were entertained by some junior officers and several attractive girls. The other guests were Generals Kurasov, Kalchenko, Vorobiev and Zheltov, and the Soviet Political Adviser, Kiselev.

We sat down at a round table. With the vodka, the abundant food, the comfortable and jovial figures of the generals, there was an atmosphere of cheerfulness and good fellowship. Centred as the dinner was around McCreery, a certain reserve was inevitable. He was friendly in his own dry manner, listened to my interpretations, smiled but said little. Winterton was restrained – it was McCreery's dinner.

Light-hearted banter between Koniev and his generals carried us through the dinner. It was clear that, apart from Zheltov, the generals were old cronies of Koniev's. They had been privates together during the First World War and he, their sergeant. Together they had risen from the ranks. Constantly their jokes referred to Koniev's humble origin. He accepted it all good-humouredly. Zheltov and Kiselev were outsiders.

Drinking was restrained, but nevertheless after a few vodkas they started telling doubtful jokes which I ignored. Koniev began quoting a famous letter sent by the Cossacks of Zaporozhie, in the time of Catherine the Great, to the Sultan of Turkey who had demanded their surrender. Parts of it are unprintable. I refused to listen and merely told McCreery what Koniev was reciting. He understood perfectly well what was going on. The Russians must have found my primness very provoking.

It was a good dinner and McCreery was flattered. As we rose to leave, Zheltov, his face flushed from the number of vodkas he had drunk, stepped up to him and burst into speech:

'Isn't it amazing that we have been able to work together! It is incredible what has been achieved! Just think how differently we were brought up and how dissimilar our education was. We might have lived our lives on different planets. Yes, and not only that, but the whole past history of our two countries, way back even before the revolution, developed on completely different lines. When I was ordered here, when I was told I was expected to work with Western Capitalist Powers and that we were to govern this country together, I thought it was an impossible task, that it would be a disaster. Yet though we quarrel and we have our differences, we have grown to respect each other's point of view, we have learnt to understand each other; and in spite of everything, we are working together and together we are governing this country. It has all been a success!'

McCreery shook him warmly by the hand. With a final toast to

Change of Commanders-in-Chief

McCreery's new appointment and a prolonged handshake between the two C-in-Cs we left.

On our return to the Schönbrunn Palace, the Press were waiting. Exhausted, Winterton stalked off, shouting over his shoulder: 'Masha, you tell them all about it.' I had been deeply moved by General Zheltov's words and the hopes they conjured up for the future. I repeated them to the Press. Later that night, listening to the BBC news bulletin, I heard my own words. I had a moment of panic wondering whether Zheltov had spoken in confidence, but there was now nothing I could do about it. I was glad the British heard what Zheltov had said, and I was pleased to see him quoted next morning in *The Times*.

The Allied Council broke up for refreshments. I turned to Marshal Koniev and asked him whether he also was leaving Vienna. He stared at me startled.

'What makes you think so?'

'You are absent-minded,' I tried to explain, 'as though mentally you were already elsewhere. I have the feeling that this may be your last Council meeting.'

He smiled, was silent, then pushing his unopened packet of cigarettes towards me, he said: 'Here is a present for you.' It was a special issue; below the Hammer and Sickle was the inscription 'For the Victors!' I kept that packet of cigarettes intact. It was the last time I saw Marshal Koniev. He had been appointed C-in-C of the Ground Forces of the Soviet Union. General Kurasov took his place.

Our new C-in-C, Lieutenant-General Sir James Stuart Steele, made his first appearance at an Allied Council meeting. Winterton introduced him all round. General Steele was a short, plump man with whitish hair cut close to the head and a long nose. He was Irish, lively and energetic. He plunged straight into the work without the usual preliminary speech-making. All went well at this his first quadrupartite conference though he spoke quietly and, sitting behind him, it was sometimes difficult to catch his opening remarks. At lunch, I sat next to him and as usual interpreted for the C-in-Cs. After the meeting Steele drew Kurasov into a separate room and offered him a cup of tea. I accompanied them. General Steele was always his natural self. He did not assert his rank nor assume any stance; he and Kurasov got along easily together.

Kurasov had not been well but he told us he was much better since he had made an important decision – not to smoke for a whole month and now he had not smoked for five days. Just before leaving, absent-mindedly he took out a cigarette. Quickly he replaced it, remarking that he must not smoke for another two weeks. As we stared at him, he laughed saying that no, he would not cheat, he must try and hold out for the whole month. Steele put his arm round him and they laughed together companionably.

When Kurasov left, Steele invited me to stay and rest awhile with him. He questioned me about my work, saying that I must let him know if there was any way he could make it easier for me. Then he asked about the Russians and what I felt about our relations with them. He listened and his questions and comments were pertinent and understanding. From what I later heard, he had made a good first impression on the other Allies.

With these two new C-in-Cs, in Vienna at least we were in good hands.

20

Something British and Good

Before his new appointment General McCreery had decided to put on some kind of a show which would be both British and good. He settled on a Tattoo. It was to take place in the gardens of the Schönbrunn Palace and any profit from it was to be donated to the children of Vienna.

Behind the Palace extensive lawns fringed by woods on either side sloped up towards the Gloriette, a triumphal arch perched high up on a hillock – the whole an ideal stage setting. Brigadier Verney, our Commandant, was put in charge. Rehearsals took place daily; bagpipes and 'Tipperary' haunted us for days on end. Verney bellowed instructions through a megaphone out of a wooden hut from which he directed operations. His voice, getting huskier every day, resounded throughout the neighbourhood. 'Fat man in the second row left. Yes, you there! What do you think you're doing? Get up, man! Get up!' Towards evening he emerged from the hut looking paler and more haggard. The strain had brought on an ulcer and as soon as the Tattoo was over Verney was to return to the UK.

The gardens and Palace surroundings were spruced up to perfection. A supreme effort had been made by all. General Steele issued invitations to the Allied C-in-Cs and the Austrian government to the Gala Opening Performance. And operation 'Henpeck' brought out the wives of our military from the UK. Now settled in Vienna they were ready to help entertain.

White Among the Reds

Two days before the Tattoo a Russian officer was murdered. We were appalled. It was a group of our soldiers who had surrounded and attacked him on a station platform. Other Russians came to his rescue and in the ensuing fighting someone had knifed him fatally. All our troops were immediately confined to barracks. So were the Soviet soldiers.

There had been several unpleasant incidents previously and the ill-feeling which had been smouldering flared up when our soldiers took part in the forcible return to the Soviet authorities of Russian soldiers who had gone over to fight on the German side. Our men knew nothing of the circumstances, but they had witnessed the men's terror and had heard reports of their mass execution.

The invitation to the Tattoo was refused by the Russian C-in-C. Relations between us were dangerously strained. The Russians made it clear they considered their C-in-C might not be safe in our hands.

I was confined to bed with a bad sore throat and no voice. I was feverish and miserable.

The telephone rang. It was General Packard's office – he was our Chief of Staff. A very important meeting was to be held that afternoon and a car would fetch me at two o'clock. Hoarsely I protested that I was in no state to interpret; I was ill and had no voice.

'General Packard says it is very urgent. You must make it,' I was told. 'You can guess what it's about. We'll bring you back immediately it's over. OK?' There was no refusing. I promised to come. I crept back into bed swallowing aspirins and sucking lozenges in an effort to get back my voice.

At two o'clock I was ready. In the conference room General Packard was pacing up and down, his hands clenched tight behind his back. Officers were perched on chairs placed all round the room and among them was Popski. I wondered why he never interpreted; he was a Russian speaker. All were awaiting the arrival of the Russians for whom chairs had been placed in the centre facing Packard's desk. Packard quickly explained to me about the Russian officer having been killed. He said a man had been arrested and would be tried. He proposed suggesting to the Russian delegate that they send their representative to see for themselves that justice was done. Packard wondered whether it would be correct to offer the delegate a drink.

Something British and Good

I told him that as Russians only drink with friends, it would be better to await the outcome of the meeting and if that were favourable, then to offer a drink. The drinks were hurriedly concealed in a cupboard. We all sat waiting in silence, conscious of the rhythm of Packard's pacing.

A Soviet general of the Justice Department, a large man with a long Jewish nose, marched in followed by his escort. Our officers jumped to their feet. The Russian saluted and sat down. His manner was icily correct. He began speaking at once. He accused our soldiers of the murder of the Russian officer and demanded that the culprit be brought to justice.

Packard hastened to admit our guilt, expressed our deep regret and stressed that we in no way condoned such an act of brutality. The culprit, he said, had been found; he had a criminal record. He had been arrested and would be tried. The other soldiers involved in the fighting, he continued, were shocked to hear of the death of this officer. Packard extended the deep sympathy of the British C-in-C. He then invited the General to send whomsoever he chose as observers to the trial.

The Russian sat still and silent for quite some time. Was he taken aback by our ready acceptance of responsibility? Had he presumed it was an act of deliberate provocation? We waited; there was no fidgeting. I had managed to interpret without coughing. I wanted to sound respectful, apologetic and convincing; my voice came out low and strained as though I were on the verge of tears. The Russian cleared his throat. He announced that he would report back to his C-in-C, but he hoped everything would be settled satisfactorily. Packard turned with an audible sigh of relief to the cupboard and asked the general whether he might offer him a drink. Out came the whisky. We waited – all eyes on the Russian. He nodded. We drank together though in silence. Then the Russians withdrew still solemn, but less frigid than on their arrival.

We might be drinking together at this higher level but among the troops the tension increased. MPs patrolled in threes and were more ostentaciously armed than usual; people refrained from lingering in dark streets alone. The great problem now was whether the Soviets would be satisfied with the arrangements made for the trial; if not,

White Among the Reds

the Russian C-in-C would certainly not come to the Tattoo and that would mean that the Russians wished to consider this an act of provocation . . . and what might that not lead to?

The day of the Tattoo it rained all morning and a strong wind blew. Anxiously we kept glancing outside. Then suddenly the rain stopped and by evening the sky was clear.

Inside the Palace everything shone and sparkled; dark green shrubs stretched up to the ceiling and huge vases of brilliantly coloured flowers lent a festive appearance. Lancers in tight parade uniforms and drawn swords were on duty and lining the ceremonial stairway. The British were all assembled, except for General Steele. As he walked in he whispered to me: 'I am glad to have you with me today.' The Americans arrived, General Mark Clark bringing his wife and daughter. Then came the French. The Austrian government drove up. I kept watch at the windows. General Steele kept coming over too. The bright conversation filling the hall sounded forced; everyone was listening as they talked. Never before had we so longed to see the Hammer and Sickle!

Then suddenly there it was in the distance on the red flags of the armoured cars and at the same time we all caught the wail of the sirens. The military police escort swept in followed by the Soviet machine-gunners, then the C-in-C's car, a line of important-looking cars carrying his generals and bringing up the rear another load of machine-gunners. The whole convoy halted in the driveway of the Palace. We drew away from the windows. General Kurasov appeared mounting the stairway, returning the Lancers' salutes and smiling admiringly at them. His generals crowded in, also wreathed in smiles. I rushed for a drink.

At the dinner preceding the Tattoo I was placed opposite General Steele, General Kurasov and Mrs Clark. Between us stood a flower arrangement lit up from within sending a multi-coloured glow down each side of the highly-polished table. Steele and Kurasov immediately fell into easy chatter. After the dessert soldiers from General Steele's own regiment piped round the table. The pipers were invited to join us at table and were introduced to Miss Clark, but their Irish brogue defeated her.

General Steele had asked me to see to the Russian C-in-C's comfort

Something British and Good

and enjoyment. During dinner I had noticed that he kept dipping into the salted almonds. I took a bag filled with them to the Tattoo. I sat behind Steele and Kurasov and in the intervals when it was dark, I handed Kurasov the bag to dip into. He munched away contentedly.

Watching some of the rehearsals by daylight we had not been impressed, but now the scene was magical, with the moonlight dappling the leaves with silver, the darkness of the woods heavy with mystery, the floodlit statues and Gloriette high-lighted in all their classical beauty. There was excitement in the contrast between the blackness around us and the brilliantly-lit stage before us.

The seats were all filled. From the moment the fireworks went off, heralding the beginning of the show, there was absolute silence. Then motorcycles roared round weaving intricate patterns, cavalry galloped headlong down the slopes, infantry marched in robot-like precision. There was a greasy-pole competition and scenes with comedians. Hundreds of white-clad athletes poured out of the woods, casting weird, symmetrical shadows as they performed their drill. The Russians had studied their programmes and knew every regiment taking part; I was inundated with questions. They praised the performance continually and the praise sounded sincere.

After each event the participants marched past the C-in-Cs who took the salute together.

It was a patriotic show. The finale, an enormous Union Jack flashing out of the darkness, engulfed everything else. It was greeted with tremendous applause. As General Kurasov praised our British troops so highly, Steele ventured to ask whether he might pass on his remarks to the soldiers concerned.

'I shall be delighted if you do this,' was Kurasov's reply. General Steele smiled and became his normal relaxed self once more.

I went three times to the Tattoo. The next time was with Alan our Consul, Colonel Gordon-Smith, our Deputy Commandant, and my friends Janet and Alec. It was fun mixing with the boisterous crowd, listening to their witticisms, sitting muffled up in rugs against the cold and munching sweets and biscuits. Janet, being Scottish, clutched us in her excitement as the Scottish pipers marched on.

The show did not run as smoothly this time. The band roared out, but nothing happened. The Scots and Irish had clashed in the woods and were having a free for all in the darkness, the MPs trying desperately to separate them. Then towards the end of the show, a floodlit ship was supposed to cross the stage to the tune of 'Rule Britannia'. But the lights fused and Britannia only ruled the darkness. Our part of the crowd relished these moments and applauded enthusiastically.

General Kurasov's wife had not come to the opening night. He asked whether he might bring her some other time. Steele was delighted and invited her for the third performance when he would be able to take her himself. Kurasov hesitated, then accepted on her behalf. Would she have the courage to go with the British C-in-C? I was to interpret for her. But before the Tattoo we were invited to dine at General Steele's. He was also entertaining General Harding, C-in-C for Trieste, and his wife. Harding would be taking the salute at the Tattoo.

As I sped along in the C-in-C's car which had come to fetch me, an equally luxurious open car caught up with us and swept past, bearing a slight, straight figure frozen into a magnificent salute. It was General Harding saluting, as he thought, the Russian C-in-C's wife. When we met on the doorstep, he was not pleased at having 'wasted such a good salute'. Kurasov's wife did not appear; we sat down without her.

After dinner General Steele took us round the garden and towards a folly, a tower with a fine view of the surrounding district. General Harding and I strolled along behind. We had started an argument. We mounted the tower still arguing. He had spoken of the Russian 'menace'; I retorted that the Russians were weak and exhausted after the war and were only interested in rebuilding their country.

'Exactly!' General Harding exclaimed. With his back to the view, he leant against the parapet to face me. 'That is precisely what I believe. And that is why we should strike now, immediately and destroy the Russians before they recover.'

I leant against the opposite parapet. The others had left the folly but we had not noticed it. For a moment I could not speak. Then I

Gen. Kurasov arriving for the Tattoo dinner at the Schönbrunn Palace.

The Author interpreting for British C-in-C, Gen. Steele, to Russian C-in-C, Gen. Kurasov, and his ADC Capt. Beloussov.

called his suggestion 'monstrous', 'unreasonable' and 'inviting trouble for the future.' We both became very heated. General Harding took it as self-evident that Russia should be destroyed. It was for him merely a question of whether it was possible to do so. He believed it was. I tried to prove it was not. 'You can't conquer the Russians,' I maintained. 'They can fall back right to the Pacific.'

General Steele came hurrying across and called up to us, reminding General Harding that he was supposed to be taking the salute at the Tattoo. We rushed down, apologising and Harding drove rapidly off.

General Steele suggested that as I was probably as tired as he was, instead of going to the Tattoo we could have a game of ping-pong and retire early to bed for a change. Gratefully I agreed.

The Vienna Area Property Control officer gave a dinner for his American, French and Russian colleagues and then took them all on to the show. I was asked to help with the Russians. This was my third visit to the Tattoo. Alan was also invited; he picked me up and brought me there. It was the last night and General McCreery had returned to take the salute.

A Russian, Major Kuzmin, his wife and their interpreter, a man who was hardly literate, sat down beside me. Kuzmin was a hearty, good-natured chap, with a rough voice and laughing eyes. Everything pleased him. As he gazed around he felt proud, he told me, that during the fighting for Vienna, special Russian units had been sent ahead to save Schönbrunn Palace from destruction. His interpreter sat down beside me and immediately went to sleep. He was drunk. The fireworks opening the show woke him up and he was sick. He went to sleep again and only woke up with the fireworks ending the show when he was sick again. But meanwhile Alan had changed places with me.

We watched McCreery taking the Salute. I had already said goodbye to him at Marshal Koniev's dinner but this was the last time we were to see him. It had been his show and it had gone excellently.

Our local crisis had subsided. Generals Steele and Kurasov were now well established in Vienna and the C-in-Cs were once more on friendly terms. But Allied Council meetings were tense. There was

Something British and Good

often complete disagreement. General Steele remained calm and reasonable, willing to examine all possibilities. But it was the UN or the Foreign Ministers' meetings that governed decisions. At one meeting with General Steele in the chair, he said to General Bethouart, the French C-in-C, that Paris must be very busy as the Foreign Ministers' conference was about to start there. After a moment's silence Steele added: 'God grant that all goes well!' The other three C-in-Cs nodded and sighed.

21

My Engagement

My personal life began to intrude. Alan dominated my thoughts. I turned to him for sympathy and companionship and I had come to rely on his complete understanding – I never needed to 'explain' the Russians to him. But now I was overwhelmed by longing for his presence.

After work we waltzed in the Kinsky Palace; we drove through the Wiener Wald by moonlight and this in spite of my already having done nine or ten hours of interpreting. We were both exhausted, it was difficult to concentrate and my thoughts strayed constantly. At last Alan proposed and I accepted. The strain of uncertainty was over.

But now I was plunged into a state of blissful intoxication in which only we two were real. Happiness is contagious. Everywhere I met with delighted exclamations and compliments. Our engagement was announced at a monster farewell party given by Jack Nicholls, Head of our Political Division, and Philip, his brother, who were both leaving for the UK. The whole Diplomatic Corps was present. Beaming ecstatically I was welcomed with smiles, handshakes and toasts by American, French and Russian diplomats as well as by our own Foreign Service officers. I had become a public figure – the British Consul's fiancée – and among these diplomats I felt at home.

The Russian ladies embraced me. Watching us dancing continually together, they heaved deep sighs.

My Engagement

One whispered to me: 'You must have been born for each other!' They said Alan resembled a Russian film star.

As for our own Britishers they were considerably relieved that I was not marrying 'one of those foreigners.'

We decided that after the wedding I would stop working. Alan had spent too many evenings waiting for a conference to end, and by the time I joined him for dinner it was cold as the gas had been turned off. It would be impossible to combine married life, the duties of a Consul's wife and the exacting work I was doing. As Alan put it: 'One tired and exasperated person in the family is more than enough.'

Meanwhile I had to continue working in order to receive food rations and accommodation in the Mess. So, though engulfed in our personal happiness, I tried to continue interpreting. At the next Allied Council meeting during lunch I whispered my news to General Steele. He seized my hand, said he was very happy and informed the other C-in-Cs. They all three shook my hand, smiling and congratulating me. They tried to persuade me to stay on as interpreter.

General Mark Clark suggested: 'Let's find fault with her Alan and have him dismissed; then she'll have to continue working.'

General Kurasov announced: 'I am very, very happy for you, and I'm coming to the wedding!' The Russian personnel around him were nodding and smiling.

The news seeped through the Commission. At a meeting of the Executive Committee where General Zheltov was insisting on seeing for himself every document under discussion, General Winterton exclaimed irritably that meetings would drag on so late that Zheltov would never have time for social life. Zheltov replied that he never went out socially – he only liked weddings – and he winked at me.

At a dinner of the Political Division a young Russian girl-interpreter asked me whether it was true that I was leaving the Commission.

'Don't you realise what this will mean to us all?' she cried. 'Don't you know how we feel about you? Couldn't you continue working after the wedding? It will be such a tragedy if you leave. Even at this small party your presence has made all the difference.'

I was deeply moved but I explained: 'I can't go on working. My duty now is to Alan. He comes first. But I shall still be in Vienna.' The girl went on trying to persuade me. She was almost in tears.

Finally, reluctantly, she gave up. 'You're so happy it's useless trying to make you think about anything else.'

General Steele and the Secretariat asked me to reconsider my decision. General Winterton also tried to persuade me, adding rather embarrassingly in front of a whole meeting: 'If you leave us, don't dare ever work for any other nationality. You are much too good.'

Mr Nott-Bower who was finally leaving Vienna added his persuasion, saying: 'The Commission is losing one of its greatest assets in you.' Encouraged by all these compliments I ventured to suggest to Mr Nott-Bower that he use his influence and tell people in London what had been achieved in Vienna and what the Russians were really like. He had met them and he knew them. He promised to do so. (But when later I met him there as Metropolitan Commissioner of Police, I was surprised to hear him expressing the same opinions of Russian inscrutability and intractability as were current in London, just as though he had never experienced Vienna. He had praised me, surely, because I helped to make it possible to work with the Russians. Then why, once in London, this rapid change of view?)

In the Interpreters' Pool I was showered with flowers. We threw a party for all the interpreters to meet Alan. Charles, the head waiter, concocted a very strong drink and somewhere he managed to scrounge some hors d'oeuvres which, in true Austrian style, he presented to Alan together with a request for a visa to Britain.

It was a rowdy party, the girls shouting 'gorko' – a Russian word meaning 'bitter' – a request to the engaged couple to sweeten the drink with a kiss. We obliged; Alan was forced to drink bottoms-up while everyone sang. We were congratulated over and over again. A speech in Russian was made by Ishkoff and was translated for Alan's benefit. This brought on more embracing and congratulating. Amidst cries of 'gorko' Alan and I escaped to my room where I was supposed to be listening for the telephone all this time, as officially I was on duty.

My work suffered; I could not put my mind to it. At a Political meeting as I sat day-dreaming my delegate made a short speech which was followed by silence. Everyone was staring at me; I had not heard a word. Padovani, the French chairman, explained that it was no

My Engagement

good expecting anything from me and he whispered to his neighbour: 'Elle a l'âme slave!'

How boring we had become! Talking about anything but ourselves was such a waste of time. A group of our Under-Secretaries arrived from Britain and I was asked to a dinner party in their honour. At table I could not resist mentioning that I had just got engaged.

There were immediate cries of dismay: 'Not to the Consul?' When I nodded, Sir Frank Newsome sighed: 'We have just spent the afternoon listening to him talking about you, and now, I suppose, we shall spend the evening listening to you singing his praises!'

When Alan proposed I was telling him about a job I had been offered by UNO. What he actually said was that he also had a job to offer me – that of his wife. He went on to say that taking first things first he would have a small but normally assured salary with a pension on retirement. We would not be rich. It was likely that the future years would be spent abroad with occasional visits to England on leave and possibly a tour of duty of a couple of years at the Foreign Office. He made it sound very prosaic. A Consul's wife, he said, does not have an easy life and I should have a lot of duties on the social side. He imagined this would be grim for me and that I would miss the excitement of what he called 'quadrupartite high-level glory'; I was confident I would enjoy it all immensely.

Meeting everyone at the Consulate was my first duty. Each member of the local Viennese staff on being introduced made a short, formal speech. All affirmed that there could be no better man than the 'Herr Konsul'. I was presented with an enormous bouquet bearing a card appropriately decorated with a waltzing couple.

Miss Klouzal, the unofficial doyenne of the Consulate, a middle-aged Austrian who had preserved the Consular carpets and it's Union Jack safely throughout the war, drew me aside. With tears in her eyes she expressed her deep regard for Alan: 'In the midst of all the chaos here, he is like a rock and though firm, he is always just,' she said with a sob in her voice.

My next duty was to meet the local British colony, among whom were numerous governesses and jockeys with a sprinkling of would-be Britishers whose fate was as yet undecided. A tea was arranged for us at the Rathaus.

White Among the Reds

Immense Union Jacks draped the whole length of the wall behind the platform on which we were to sit at a long table. About two hundred people were present. At our entry they rose to their feet; the ladies whipped out lorgnettes. Alan whispered to me not to touch the food; it would later be divided among those with children.

The table was laden with presents. Photographers flashed cameras. A few days previously at the Consulate a parcel was brought in from a petitioner. Alan waved it away saying brusquely that presents were not acceptable. Miss Klouzal and I peeped inside; it was a box inlaid with bamboo with the year and Alan's initials engraved on it. Inside was an ivory Majong set. Now there it lay among the wedding gifts on the table before us and Alan was expressing fulsome thanks to the giver.

Alan made a speech. Then as we left, myself sheltering behind numerous bouquets of flowers, the colony burst into 'For He is a Jolly Good Fellow' in ancient and somewhat cracked voices.

Miss Klouzal saying good-bye added: 'I am always called the mother of the colony, but now you are its queen!'

I learnt that in the Foreign Service I would have to keep my mouth shut. We were bidden to lunch with Mr Mack, our Political Adviser and Alan's boss. The luncheon was for the Austrian Foreign Minister, Herr Gruber, and his wife. It was to be a big affair, a pompous occasion and it was a 'must'. In the Foreign Service, Alan informed me, invitations from those in higher grades were never refused.

The usual buzz of conversation broke out as we sat down to lunch. Small talk was bandied back and forth interspersed with light, self-conscious laughter. I found I was seated next to Herr Gruber himself, a tall, handsome man with gracious manners. This was a rare opportunity. Here was a highly-placed Minister of the Austrian government; I could appeal to him direct. Could the Austrians not take advantage of the occupation? Could they not contribute towards understanding between East and West? Must they keep trying to set the Allies at each others' throats? We had quite a heated argument, Herr Gruber and I. It was most stimulating. I did not realise that Alan was listening anxiously at the other end of the table. He was able to catch only a word or two here and there, but that was apparently enough to cause him considerable unease. He explained later that Foreign Service personnel (and this included wives) are supposed to express only the views of their government and they must be careful never to meddle or even appear to meddle in the internal affairs of the country in which they are stationed. Lesson number one, but I was in no condition to take it seriously.

Michael Burn, of *The Times*, arranged for us to dine with three local correspondents of the Soviet News Agency, *Tass*. They wished to meet me, the great-grandchild of their Russian hero, the Decembrist, Ivan Poustchine. The Smolletts of the *Daily Express* were among others invited. We all met in the Kinsky Palace.

I disappointed the *Tass* correspondents. For the famous man's great-grandchild to choose to marry a Britisher and to prefer the British way of life was incomprehensible. They kept enquiring why I did not return to the 'Motherland' and what in Britain was it that attracted me so? This was difficult to explain. Finally I told them how before the war my mother and I were proposing to join other members of the family in America, but when war came and German bombs fell on London, we suddenly felt that nothing should drive us away; we were Londoners, we belonged there and there we would stay.

One of the *Tass* correspondents had been stationed in London during the blitz. His colleague was curious to know what it had been like. What struck him most, he replied, were the number of beggars in the streets of London.

The Russians kept making remarks aside in Russian forgetting that I understood. Embarrassed they lapsed into silence. One of them exclaimed: 'You see, we cannot think of you as one of "them"; we keep forgetting you are not one of "us"!'

Nevertheless they drank our health numerous times. As soon as the word 'gorko' cropped up Alan whisked me off onto the dance floor.

The evening ended with all of us singing 'Auld Lang Syne.'

White Among the Reds

As a result of this dinner the *Daily Express* carried a news item about our wedding; in seven lines there were six errors!

I had attended my last Internal Affairs meeting. As our last social duty Alan and I gave a dinner in the Kinsky Palace for its Chairman, Brigadier Block, his wife and his daughter, Ann. Block wanted us to invite his Russian colleagues; we invited Colonel Ilichev and Lieut-Colonel Miasnikov and their wives, stressing that we would be delighted if they came, but would understand if they were unable to do so. They accepted. So far, though they invariably accepted invitations, they had never turned up at any private dinner.

The evening started with drinks. We were a large company and soon all were assembled except for the Russians. I went down to the soldiers on duty at the entrance and asked them to direct the Russians upstairs. We served more and more drinks as we waited . . . and waited . . . In spite of everyone else's pessimism I was sure they would come. But soon it was so late we had to go into dinner.

I took a final look round the hall and hurried to the top floor to the ladies' room. When I opened the door, there on the sofa sat the Russian officers and their wives! From the look on my face they must have realised something was very wrong. They explained that the soldier below had jerked his thumb upwards so up they went as high as they could. Not finding anyone around they had settled down in here. They wondered why so many women kept entering the room and retreating rapidly. When I explained they burst out laughing, then considering this unseemly they controlled themselves and we proceeded downstairs.

Mrs Block and Ann had never met Russians before; they were excited. And it was the first time that Ilichev and Miasnikov had been in the Kinsky Palace. It was a boisterous party, everyone friendly and relaxed.

Mr Nott-Bower joined us as he still had not left. Ilichev told him: 'I have never learnt so much from anyone as I have from you. I feel deeply grateful.' The Russians kept looking round at the sumptious and elegant surroundings, the smartly-uniformed officers, the gen-

My Engagement

eral air of decorum. Maisnikov leant across to me and remarked that they had forgotten what gracious living meant.

At my last Allied Council meeting General Steele made a speech referring to my 'Swan Song'. Though flustered and excited, I managed to get through it. Afterwards General Steele announced that unfortunately he would be away on the day of our wedding, August 17th, and he was very sad to miss it. General Kurasov tried to persuade him to return in time, but Steele explained that he had to attend an important conference and it would be quite impossible for him to get back by that date. Strictly speaking Steele's absence precluded Kurasov's coming as at any British function the British C-in-C should always be present to receive any of the other C-in-Cs. But if Kurasov did come, he would arrive as was his usual custom with armoured-carloads of machine-gunners and accompanied by a galaxy of generals to whom invitations had been sent just in case. Quite a problem for our Military Police!

At the doors of the Inter-Allied Secretariat, with a great deal of handshaking and more expressions of appreciation, General Steele thanked me warmly while I tried to express my gratitude for all their kindness. I was flattered and exhilarated by so many compliments. I was in a kind of glorious haze. Outside orders were suddenly barked out, the Guard of Honour came briskly to attention, the band struck up the National Anthem and I stepped triumphantly out in front of the C-in-Cs.

General Steele thrust me gently aside, saying: 'No, dear, this is now for me.'

We now had to arrange the wedding. Alan had agreed to a private religious ceremony in the Russian church and this was to be followed by a reception at Sachers Hotel. We also had to be married in an Austrian Registry Office.

Colonel Gordon-Smith, who was to give me away, was insisting on a white wedding and I agreed happily. Alec would be best man. But

White Among the Reds

when we made these decisions we were not very practical; we did not consider what would, in the circumstances, be possible.

The Russian priest at first was most helpful, but when he realised that I would be given away by the acting Commandant himself, his tune changed; here was a chance to benefit the whole of his parish! He insisted on a full choir, which included members of the Opera House, and demanded exorbitant prices in NAAFI goods for the ceremony. We only received our personal NAAFI rations but Alec and Ishkov undertook to produce the necessary and to deal with the priest. They bargained over each item. The priest knew the exact black market value of whisky, gin, soap, cigarettes and chocolate. Money was useless.

As I waited for the bargaining to end I glanced through the Marriage Register. There was a long list of Soviet soldiers marrying Austrian, catholic girls. Some of the men had given their religion as Moslem. The priest saw me looking. He asked sadly who else would bless their union if he refused?

Alec mentioned that my mother was unable to send the traditional ikon for the wedding. The priest asked which Ikon I preferred of those hanging on the walls of the church. I pointed to a Virgin and Child. He took it down and handed it to me, shaking his head at Alec, who was offering to pay for it. So in spite of the church wedding being private we were to have a full choir and all the customary ceremonial.

The reception and my clothes for the wedding were the next problems to be tackled.

Though none of our relations or friends would be able to come out from the UK, our invitation list for the reception had grown to some four hundred guests. All food in Vienna was rationed. Alan drew his food rations from the army. Extra food could only be released by the army for official entertainment and our wedding was hardly that. There was no way, it seemed, to obtain food for the reception.

General Winterton came to our rescue. A chit arrived from him giving permission for rations to be released for two hundred and fifty persons for what was termed for the sake of legality 'H.M. Consul's

My Engagement

Inter-Allied Cocktail Party'. We hurried over to Sacher's. The sergeant in charge of catering there had already agreed to help us as soon as clearance was given for the food. The numbers specified did not worry him; once he had that bit of paper he could do what he liked. He would provide a buffet luncheon and his assistant, Antoinette, would take charge of the flower decorations and the artistic side of the catering; the flowers would come from the Palace hot-house.

As we sipped the cocktails Antoinette provided, we learnt from the corporal of the complications of catering for local VIPs; General Mark Clark wouldn't touch anything with tomatoes in it and Marshal Koniev only ate eggs; invariably all the eggs provided would be snatched up by someone else. He told us how the head waiter who had a habit of talking to himself dropped all the potato crisps under the C-in-C's chair. As he collected them he muttered away to himself: 'Now come along little crisps, get right inside.' Someone later remarked: 'What a good way that was of passing the message to the C-in-C. Who would have thought of it!'

There now remained the problem of my clothes. I had no coupons with which the buy clothes in the UK. The only possibility of obtaining anything, was through friends going on leave to Italy or Czechoslovakia. Thus I acquired a few items of flimsy and frivolous underwear and, more important, blue silk material for a going-away costume. But the real problem was the wedding dress.

Alan had suggested tentatively that: 'One of those pretty summer dresses you wear would do, wouldn't it?' No, I told him firmly, it would not do.

The Polish Countess, Irene Russocky, a heroine of the Polish underground, whom we had met through Colonel Gordon-Smith and who was to be seen most evenings floating around in a dazzlingly white evening dress in the Kinsky Palace, introduced me to her own dressmaker, the famous Herr Schubert. She explained that most things could be had in Vienna if one knew where to look. She was Vienna-born and as she termed it, 'knew everyone'. In the sacred portals of Herr Schubert's establishment, where his name was pronounced in respectful whispers, we were met with 'Frau Gräfin' here

White Among the Reds

and 'Frau Gräfin' there and a profuse kissing of hands and curtsying. Irene countered with 'Herr Konsul' pronounced often, loud and clear. I was promised that everything would be ready on time so long as I could produce the material for the wedding dress. We decided on crêpe-satin. Herr Schubert himself drew up the sketch for it and I was measured.

Unobtrusively Irene mentioned the blue silk material for my going-away costume and somehow it was agreed that this also would be ready on time.

There were now eleven days to go before the wedding and no one was due for any leave either in Italy or Czechoslovakia. Where were we to get the material for the wedding dress?

General Morgan, who had replaced General Alexander in Italy as C-in-C of the Central Mediterranean Forces, arrived in Vienna and General Steele invited me to a dinner-dance in his honour. During the dinner, I launched into the only subject of interest – my wedding and my wedding dress.

General Morgan interrupted me. 'What exactly is it that you can't get?' I told him – the material for my wedding dress. He called down to his ADC who was seated at the bottom end of the table and ordered him to get whatever it was I needed as soon as they returned to Italy.

After dinner a nervous ADC took details of the kind of material I needed and the amount required. He promised to do his best and to have it sent up to Vienna as quickly as possible.

A few days later our ADCs' office rang me up. Down the phone an officer hummed Mendlesson's Wedding March and then informed me that General Steele had received a roll of white satin material which had been flown up by devious routes from the HQ at Caserta in Italy and would it, by any chance, have anything to do with me?

I rushed over to collect it and Alan had it delivered immediately to Herr Schubert. All was now under control.

22

Our Wedding

The great day, August 17th, arrived. The sun was shining and I had my white wedding.

Christine, my Austrian maid, woke me with breakfast in bed and a wedding present – a bunch of flowers in a deep green vase made in the factory where her daughter worked, with her daughter's own mark on it.

Janet and Irene burst into my room. Janet, my earliest friend in Vienna, was to act as Maid of Honour. Irene, my Polish benefactress who produced Herr Schubert, the dressmaker, now brought me a hat, gloves and purse for my going-away costume. They both helped me to dress. When I was ready and stood up in my wedding dress I felt on top of the world. It was worked on the matt side and was fastened with tiny buttons in front from the waist to the neck; it was close fitting at the neck and had long sleeves and a small train. I felt regal.

In the mirror I watched Irene and Janet, nervous and tense, glaring and snapping at each other above my head as Irene struggled with the hairpins to pin up my veil; Janet was passing them to her but she kept dropping them. They both looked so fierce, I laughed. The tension broke and we all felt less nervous. The veil was finally fixed. Gazing proudly at me Irene called me a model bride. She kissed and hugged me disturbing my hair and veil. Christine and her daughter looked on sighing romantically.

White Among the Reds

Colonel Gordon-Smith hovered behind the door till finally admitted. He greeted me formally with the ikon and bread and salt in true Russian fashion. He had sent me my bouquet beforehand. It consisted of four different kinds of orchids; big white ones and big green and white ones forming the bouquet itself with sprays of small blue orchids and a spray of small white ones cascading down and in a curve across my dress. Colonel Gordon-Smith was imposing in his uniform, but he had a cheerful grin on his face.

We swept downstairs and all had a glass of wine. We sallied forth, Gordon-Smith carrying the ikon, I the bouquet and Janet my train. Janet also had to keep lifting up the strap of my sandal as it slipped off my heel. The interpreters cheered us on our way.

The official Commandant's car and our army driver in beret and with medals both sparkled with polish. At the Austrian registry office, the car had to draw up beside mounds of debris. We picked our way through, entered the building and mounted two flights of dismal, uncarpeted stairs past staring groups of Austrians and into a spacious room decorated with flowers where Alan, very serious, and Alec, grinning, were already waiting. The Standesbeamter stood behind a table in a long black robe; Alan and I placed ourselves before him.

The Standesbeamter first asked us whether we truly wished to be married. In a short speech he stressed the difficulties of the marriage contract. Then he married us. Mr Taylor, the Vice-Consul and Alan's temporary replacement, made sure that all was legal. Alec took numerous photos of the ceremony and continued snapping us throughout the morning at both opportune and inopportune moments. Janet fussed with my train and veil. Outside Alec insisted on photographing us all including the driver in front of the heaps of rubble for 'local colour'.

Alan and I parted and drove separately to the church. As I waited outside in the car (the priest, being Russian, was late), an Austrian bride approached on foot. She look frightened and pathetic in dark clothing. She was accompanied by a few dismal-looking relatives and she was holding some flowers that were already wilting. Colonel Gordon-Smith suggested I give her one of my orchids for luck. I handed it to her through the car window. She immediately responded with a smile and gave me one of her flowers. Gordon-Smith also took a piece of coal off a coal-merchant who was passing. That, he said, would bring me good luck too.

As I joined Alan in the church the choir burst into rich, joyful melody. The church was resplendent with white flowers, and with the glistening vestments of the priest. Only a few of our friends were present, among them Olia, Irene and Ishkoff, but, as the church doors were open, soldiers and Austrians crowded in off the street. Alan and I held lighted candles; several friends, including Alec and Ishkoff took turns to hold golden crowns above our heads. We drank from the same vessel, exchanged rings and were led by the priest, his hand over our clasped hands, round the small altar. For Alan's benefit the priest said some of the prayers in German. In his sermon he also stressed the difficulties of married life with an exhortation to us, when in trouble, to read the New Testament. Alan had to say 'I do' (Zhelau) in Russian.

In the middle of the service the churchwarden was seen advancing across the church struggling with a heavy suitcase which emitted sounds of clinking glass – the NAAFI goods – our payment to the choir and the priest.

After the service the priest led us up to the Ikonastas or Golden Gates which shut off the main altar. He motioned us to kiss the ikons on its doors while he explained the figures of saints depicted on them.

When we came out white flowers and ribbons on the car were fluttering in the wind. We swept through Vienna to Sacher's. Antionette, the catering assistant, had done a wonderful job. The long table in the centre of the dining-room, laden with good things, was an artistic achievement. In the centre the three-tier wedding cake was covered with real icing-sugar. Waiters were rushing about with trays. Flowers were everywhere.

We stood close together, happy and tense, at the entrance to the dining-room in an alcove framed by a mass of greenery. Beside us a table overflowed with flowers from friends. We shook hands for about three quarters of an hour. Irene fluttered around arranging my dress while photographers snapped away. Alan kept saying: 'Thank you so much!' before the guests had had time to make their little speeches. General Cherrière, the French Deputy C-in-C, came with his wife and her usual suite of ladies. General Winterton brought his son who

White Among the Reds

was in naval uniform and presented us with a cut glass bowl. The interpreters were present in force. Only four Russians turned up, all in mufti, and no C-in-C. One Russian girl-interpreter whom I had repeatedly tried to persuade into an evening dress, but who had been too bashful and modest and had always appeared at evening parties in uniform, had finally taken the plunge. In our honour she now appeared in a sleeveless evening gown with décolletage. It was fortunate that mine was a long dress too to keep her company.

Everyone was in good spirits, quite literally so, by the time we joined them. I noticed the priest and churchwarden concentrating fully on the food at a separate small table. Mr Mack, Alan's boss, proposed the toast. We cut the cake. Then we disappeared to change and have a quick drink on our own. When we came down again, we hurried through a shower of rose petals. Outside the crowd was even greater.

A Russian officer stepped smartly up. It was Captain Beloussov, the Russian Commander-in-Chief's ADC. In English he said: 'I have been commanded in the name of General Kurasov to present you with this with his very best wishes and congratulations.' He saluted and handed us a huge, square, colourfully-decorated basket filled with flowers, mostly gladioli, thrusting out in all directions. In the centre stood a bottle of Russian champagne flanked by large slabs of Russian chocolate (my weakness). Photographers hurried up. Beaming we were taken from all angles with the basket and the Russian officer.

We climbed into the official car, the basket placed before us; General Steele's ADC then handed me a letter. It was a charming note from General Steele thanking me once again and congratulating us. At the military HQ we changed into Alan's more modest car squeezing the basket in with us. And off we drove to Styria for our honeymoon.

This had been my day; the bridegroom, in Alan's words, 'having been essential but inconspicuous.'

Exhausted, we drove to Mariazell, a village where rooms were booked for us in the Hotel Laufenstein. We were led into a couple

Our Wedding

of dark, dreary rooms. Alan began to protest but the word 'Konsul' in big letters on the car had already galvanised the hotel manager into shifting us rapidly into his best suite with a corner room and balcony overlooking on one side the village square with its huge cathedral and on the other the mountains.

We hastened to report to the local British garrison consisting of two officers and some thirty men of a Yorkshire regiment as they were to provide us with additional rations; the hotel could supply little in the way of food. The military were not forthcoming. They resented our intrusion into what had so far been exclusively their preserve. They said vaguely that they would see what they could produce.

Early next morning the two officers were announced. They came in grinning and thrust the *Union Jack*, the army newspaper, at us. There we were on the front page with Kurasov's ADC and the basket of flowers. The officers had brought milk, eggs, butter and cheese, all marvellously fresh. We had a delicious breakfast on the balcony watching the activities in the village square below. Lorries clattered across the cobbles to the door of the cathedral bringing pilgrims. We later learnt that they were childless couples arriving from all over the country to pray for fecundity.

Mariazell lay in a hollow surrounded by hills with only two dangerously steep roads climbing up and over them. We were cut off from the rest of the world, in our own cosy corner. We bathed in the local lake, left the car with an army patrol at the bottom of a hill, climbed it and lazed on its summit eating wild strawberries, raspberries and bilberries. Since our photograph had appeared in the paper the local army detachment could not do enough for us. The officers and sergeant dropped in on us for drinks arriving in a jeep at a speed that sent all the populace and the hens flying in all directions. On Alan's birthday they gave us a magnificent spread for dinner culminating in so rich a birthday cake, smothered in cream and strawberries, that it kept us awake most of that night.

One wet afternoon the commander asked Alan whether he would speak to the men on the Foreign Service and would I afterwards answer questions about the Russians? We agreed. Alan produced his usual talk for such occasions and we were told that since the men had

White Among the Reds

kept quiet, had not yawned, shuffled their feet, or talked among themselves we could take it that they had been interested. They were also swilling beer most of the time! When my turn came and I was asked questions about the Russian generals and their ways, to my surprise and embarrassment I found myself constantly appealing to Alan. I had always previously spoken unselfconsciously, but now I found I was lost for words and hesitant. I no longer reacted spontaneously without considering the impression I was making on others. I was now the 'Consul's wife'; I was inhibited by the aura of the Foreign Service that hung over us.

But when it transpired that, though our soldiers shared the frontier with the Russians, they had never had anything to do with them and only glared at each other from their respective frontier posts, I forgot myself at last and exclaimed: 'But that is ridiculous!'

'What can we do?' one of them asked. 'They don't speak English; we don't speak Russian. And they may not want to have anything to do with us.'

'Why don't you invite them to a game of football?' I suggested. 'They'll jump at that.' The soldiers liked the idea and several of them murmured: 'OK, we'll try.'

A few days later the officers reported what had occurred. The two sides had met and all was informality and fun till the ball burst.

The British team ran with it to the local shoemaker. He shook his head, he had no leather, he couldn't mend the ball. Disconsolately they returned to the field. The Russians seized the ball, ran back to the shoemaker and thrust their rifles in his face. He produced the leather and the ball was mended. Laughing, the two sides continued a somewhat unorthodox and rowdy game.

On rainy days we watched the pilgrims in the square. There had been no pilgrimages since 1939. Now they were arriving daily and processed towards the cathedral chanting dolefully.

On the last morning the clanging of bells woke us at half past seven. Lorries were already arriving; we counted thirty. It was a special celebration. A procession formed up with banners unfurled in the wind and wound its way round the cathedral singing lustily to the accompaniment of an orchestra. At the same time the village band struck up a lively march as part of their weekly concert at the other

The Author's wedding in the Russian Orthodox Church in Vienna.

Capt. Beloussov presenting the Author with a wedding present from the Russian C-in-C, Gen. Kurasov.

end of the square. We were caught midway between the two competing village orchestras.

Our Austrian honeymoon was over so quickly and we flew on to London for a month's further leave.

There the euphoria continued as we were welcomed and entertained by each other's relatives and friends. Wherever we went presents were thrust upon us. There was only one distressing incident when a White Russian lady, a very old friend of my parents, on whom we wished to call, refused to receive us. She had read in *The Times* a piece about our wedding and my work with the Soviets. I had associated with communists; she never wished to see me again. But intoxicated as I was with happiness I could not feel the hurt for long.

Back we drove to Vienna, I now as the British Consul's wife.

23

Last Days in Vienna

At the British zone frontier it was the Austrian police who examined our papers and on entering the Soviet zone Austrian police accompanied the Russian military; also there were noticeably fewer soldiers around – control was passing into Austrian hands.

Over dinner that night Alec reported many changes in Vienna. In the ACA the Russian military were being replaced by Political Commissars. When General Zheltov, the Deputy C-in-C, was absent from the Executive Committee it was the Head of the Economic Division, a Political Commissar, who replaced him not General Morozov, the Chief of Staff, though the latter was his senior in rank.

Preparations were under way for the signing of the peace treaty with Austria, he told us. This would mean the total withdrawal of Allied forces from the country. The Commission was dwindling rapidly. More and more of our officers were going home and the Russians were withdrawing behind their so-called Iron Curtain. But here Alec told us that during an Allied Conference in Moscow Marshal Koniev, now Commander-in-Chief of the Soviet Ground Forces, had sought out and entertained every Britisher with whom he had had any contact in Vienna, even the most junior official. This was good to hear.

As the British Consul's wife I now only met Russians at official functions. They greeted our return with warmth and smiles and were ready to listen to all the delights of our honeymoon holiday. I was immediately drawn into entertaining them and interpreting for them.

Alan was remarkably good-natured about it; he assured me that he enjoyed their company – they were so refreshingly unpredictable – and the knowledge that these contacts would soon cease enhanced the pleasure they gave us.

The Austrian Government's reception at the Hofburg to celebrate the 950th anniversary of the birth of Austria started with a concert. Alan and I were threading our way to our seats at the back of the hall when General Steele, our C-in-C, in the front row, restlessly turning this way and that, spied us and waved. His ADC came hurrying over. Would we come and sit behind General Steele and General Kurasov, the Russian C-in-C, who were unable to converse as General Steele only had a German interpreter with him. We went up front. General Kurasov, handsome and smiling as ever, sighed and said to me: 'I don't know what I shall do without you!'

Steele hurried in with: 'But she is mine, not yours!' They laughed and settled down to their usual chatter. I interpreted with Alan beside me by no means loath to be seated with the C-in-Cs.

As the British were presiding in the ACA both General Steele and General Winterton, his Deputy, threw large parties. General Steele gave a private dance in his house. He was an excellent host. He expected and saw to it that everyone from the British element contributed his share to the general enjoyment and the men were not allowed to congregate round the bar. 'If you didn't enjoy a party,' he would say, 'it was because you did not make that party a success.'

The Allies were there in force, the rooms full of senior officers. Alan and I took care of General Kurasov who was in fine form.

A few days before he had been invested with a Hungarian Order. 'My daughter – she is eleven – insisted on getting an Order too,' he told us. 'I could not control her. She caused utter confusion and dismay in the Hungarian cabinet. Imagine my embarrassment! In the end, her mother was found and she carried her off in disgrace.' He smiled proudly. When Alan strolled off to greet some of the ladies, General Kurasov told me: 'You have chosen well. He is a fine man, your husband.'

There was a conjuror. We crowded into the drawing-room to watch

Last Days in Vienna

him perform. He turned out to be a superb pickpocket. He warned an officer, whom he drew out into the centre of the room, that he was going to steal his watch. He then launched into a string of amusing stories passing rapidly from one to the other, weaving them around the personality of the officer whom he prodded and slapped in illustration, thus distracting the officer's and everyone else's attention. Simultaneously, with a succession of lightning-swift thrusts with one hand at the officer's wrist, he gradually loosened the watch-strap till the watch fell into his hand. Hardly anyone noticed these rapid jabs; we were enjoying his jokes at the expense of the officer. There was amazement when he dangled the watch before the officer's nose. He kept glancing at his bare wrist.

The conjuror removed General Steele's tie and the Danish Minister's braces without them noticing though both men had watched him in action on the officer. He also produced twelve ping-pong balls out of his mouth, followed by an egg. He warned one guest, Mr Bell, to keep a tight hold on his watch by placing his hand over it. He then proceeded to remove the contents of his pockets without Mr Bell's realising it. When finally he handed the numerous articles back amidst general laughter, the astonished Mr Bell let go his watch to stretch out both hands to retrieve his possessions. The next moment the watch was in the conjuror's hand.

As a finale he warned us all to keep an eye on our watches. He started off round the room slapping people on the back, joking, teasing and prodding them. As he patted the arm of a Russian officer beside me, I was amused to hear the latter whisper: 'Don't touch my inside pocket!'

Having done the round of the room he stopped in front of General Kurasov. The General was leaning back, relaxed in his armchair, his hands along its arms. The conjuror asked him in Russian: 'May I?' and thrust his hand into Kurasov's jacket pocket. Out came a wrist watch, then another and another. Plunging into the other pocket he brought out more and more watches. He was finally holding about twenty. Kurasov was dumbfounded. Silence fell on the company. Jokes about the Russian passion for stealing watches were all very well but to make a fool in public of the Russian C-in-C . . . We all watched Kurasov, Steele most anxiously. After a moment's hesitation

White Among the Reds

Kurasov shrugged his shoulders, opened wide his arms as though to protest his innocence and rising, slapped the conjuror hard (and painfully) on the back and burst out laughing. Steele also had risen. He approached Kurasov clapping loudly and smiling broadly. The whole room applauded laughing with relief.

It was even funnier when the conjuror returned each watch to its owner all around the room. They clasped their bare wrists with astonishment. Kurasov was able to get his own back. This was the last we saw of General Kurasov.

General Winterton gave a dinner-dance for the Allies. As we came in he whispered: 'The Russians are here. You will look after them, won't you?'

We decided to get in a bit of dancing first. In the Paul Jones I stopped opposite Herr Figl, the Austrian Prime Minister. He was tiny and was dismayed at my height. But when he found that I understood German he whirled me expertly off into a Viennese waltz.

We were sitting with a Russian General and his ADC when General Morozov, the Russian Chief of Staff, entered with his young daughter, Valya. She was plump, dimpled and cheerful. She wore an evening dress with a modest neck-line and very little make-up. There was no coquetry about her; she smiled at everyone in the same manner. Morozov immediately remarked that I was putting on weight and he reminded me that all Russian women tended to do so. 'You must take up sport,' he advised. Then he exclaimed: 'You have become very Grande Dame-like!'

General Winteron asked us to take them all into dinner. As we tucked into the good food, Alan got a thorough dose of Russian though every now and then Morozov barked out a remark in English at him. Morozov smoked the whole time. Valya, who neither smoked nor drank, waved the smoke away with her hand and complained that her father's cigarettes made her head ache.

When we reached the dessert stage, Morozov started grumbling: 'You women! You fill yourselves with all this cream and chocolate. Show some restraint! Look at all these women round you; they take dainty helpings. They don't stuff themselves with all this rich food.

And look what figures they have, slim, elegant, charming!' Valya gave him a mischievous smile and helped herself to another chocolate éclair. I did too.

'Papa!' she suddenly turned to her father. 'I was told that you called on the priest.'

'So?'

'But did you?'

'Yes, I did.'

'Papa, you didn't! I can't believe it! What for?'

'In the course of my duties.'

'But I thought priests went out with the Middle Ages! I just can't believe it!' I watched them as they teased each other and hardly realised that when we said good-bye we should never see them again.

Alec had also met Valya and thought highly of her. He maintained that only Russian women were completely natural. He also maintained, and I agreed with him, that among Europeans only Russians were truly democratic at heart. Differences in wealth and position were more noticeable in the Red Army than in ours, but though the Soviet general might have eleven cars and numerous servants, though he might treat his soldiers harshly, nevertheless, the servants and soldiers answered him back on equal terms. There was no servility.

I was driving once in a Russian general's car when he told the driver to take a certain short cut. The driver exclaimed: 'Every time we come this way you tell me to take this short cut and every time we get lost. I know the way, you don't. You have your job, I have mine. So let us go my way and no more short cuts.' The general agreed.

It was amazing how British people like Alec who learnt Russian, were constantly in touch with them, knew more of their faults than others, were irresistably drawn towards them and towards all things Russian.

Our new visa officer, George Berry, had worked for many years in the Soviet Union. He claimed to know all about the Russians and was always warning others to beware of them. Yet at a dinner we attended in his flat, together with Colonel Gordon-Smith and Alec, the whole evening was devoted to listening to Russian music and to looking at slides of the Soviet Union. George, Gordon-Smith and Alec kept

White Among the Reds

lapsing into Russian as they reminisced at length. They finally burst into Russian song, waking Alan who not being quite so enamoured with all things Russian, had dozed off comfortably.

The former Russian Archbishop Sergius of Prague had been transferred by the Soviet authorities to Vienna. He was White Russian, with an aristocratic background and here he was in Soviet hands. The old priest had been safe enough while the military were in command but now that they were relinquishing power . . . I decided I had better call on the Archbishop as soon as possible. Alan raised no objection.

The address I had was in the Russian zone of Vienna. I had never before been there on my own and on foot. A chaffeur-driven car, I thought, would attract attention which might not be welcome to the Archbishop.

This part of the city was shabby and depressing; it had suffered the greatest battering during the fighting. Soviet soldiers elbowed their way through the crowds. I saw one Russian officer slouching along, his cap askew, pushing his way roughly through the civilians. As he passed, an Austrian policeman saluted him. In an instant the officer was transformed. His back straight, his cap at the correct angle, he returned a smart salute and continued on his way politely without pushing. Somewhat reassured I nevertheless hurried along as fast as I could.

Then I realised I was being followed. I stopped and gazed into a shop window; the footstops I had become aware of ceased also. Without turning I could make out a man gazing into a shopwindow not far behind. I walked on; the footsteps started up again. Repressing my fear and an irrational repugnance for the whole situation, I searched for the house-number I wanted. As I stopped the footsteps quickened and a dark-coated figure brushed rapidly past and entered the house I was seeking. It was dilapidated with uncarpeted stone steps leading upwards. As I entered I could hear my follower now clambering up ahead of me. I followed, stopped on the second floor and knocked. The footsteps had gone on higher up.

The Archbishop himself opened the door. He was an impressive-looking little man with a straggly beard, in a monk's long black garments and circular hat with a black veil hanging at the back.

I introduced myself. He invited me in. I kissed his hand, as he blessed me. We were in an almost empty room, with only a table covered by a white cloth and several hard wooden chairs. There was tea on the table; he offered me a cup and gave me a saucer full of jam and a spoon. We ate and drank exchanging remarks about the cold weather. The Archbishop had a high-pitched voice and a habit of playing with his beard. I now saw that he was a very old man. His garments had taken on a brown hue; the sleeves were frayed at the cuffs. But the gold cross hanging on a thick gold chain round his neck was studded with real gems.

I explained more fully my position. He made no comment. A door into the next room was half open. I longed to ask him whether he was all right, whether it was wise for me to visit him, whether there was anything I could do to help him. I wanted to know how the Soviet authorities were treating him. Just as I decided to risk a question someone sneezed behind that open door. The Archbishop gave no sign of having heard. I lapsed into silence.

I was uneasy and nervous; I asked whether I might smoke.

'It is not correct to smoke in the presence of a bishop,' was his answer. Then seeing my confusion, for I knew this perfectly well, he smiled and added: 'I often hear stamping outside my door. Then I know that a Soviet officer is putting out his cigarette before entering. They show respect.'

I rose to go. He blessed me again as I kissed his hand. At the door he suddenly said: 'Come again. I knew your grandfather. We were young men together. We had a good time. We'll talk about it sometime.'

I hurried down those steps, followed as I knew I would be, then out into the street. I almost ran back to the British zone.

Around Christmas one evening our maid Ike announced a 'Herr Struve'. I had known Arkadi Struve many years before as a theological student. Now as he entered I recognised his long ascetic face and unkempt appearance. He had accompanied the Archbishop who, he said, was outside and might they call on us?

Alan hurried out to greet the Archbishop. He entered looking solemn with a heavy, distant expression on his face – an official look. As he crossed the threshold he made the Sign of the Cross and in a loud tenor began chanting a Christmas hymn, Arkadi taking up the base part. Thus singing, they entered the drawing-room, an astonished Alan trailing along behind, and there being no ikon (mine was in the bedroom) they faced the Christmas tree. The Archbishop said a prayer and blessed our flat.

I introduced Alan, and Ike brought in tea, biscuits, cakes and sandwiches. I asked her to bring saucers of jam too. We settled into armchairs and exchanged remarks rather formally. But once it was clear that we were not going to ask any unwelcome questions, and once they had relieved their obvious hunger, our guests relaxed. We were soon chatting in a mixture of French, Germany and Russian. Arkadi, who was very deaf, politely attempted to interpret for Alan. As the Archbishop talked about my grandfather and the fun they had had together, he had quite a twinkle in his eye. His high-pitched laugh resounded continually; he obviously enjoyed a good gossip. Arkadi, he told us, had accompanied him from Prague and now acted as his secretary, cook, housemaid, acolyte in church or whatever else was needed.

There was some confusion when they spoke of 'we'. Occasionally they were referring to the White Russian community and sometimes to the Red Army to which the Archbishop was now officially attached. He told us a little about themselves; he said that both he and Arkadi were all right. In any case at his age what had he to fear? His church had been repaired by the Red Army, it was heated and a car had been put at his disposal. It was the chauffeur who had sneezed behind the door. This young man had been attached to him presumably in order to watch and report on him. But he was a Yugoslav and spoke no Russian. Here the Archbishop laughed heartily.

'Typically Russian, isn't it? To put a man to eavesdrop who doesn't understand the language!'

He told us that the chauffeur's mother inundated him with letters from Yugoslavia. She was saddened that her son had become a communist, an atheist and was delighted that he was now attached to the Archbishop and might thus come under his influence. Meanwhile the young man brought them logs from the woods, cleaned out their stove and generally made himself useful. So much we were told but a great deal more was left unsaid.

When they departed, Arkadi reluctantly accepting a bagful of food, Alan escorted them to the car. There to his astonishment stood his own chauffeur who had recently disappeared. He had been screened by our Security before getting the job with Alan but now here he was, the Archbishop's chauffeur, assigned to him by the Soviet authorities. Embarrassed, the young man nevertheless smiled as he saluted Alan.

One evening Alan burst into our flat and announced: 'It's Baghdad!' I didn't understand. 'What about Baghdad?'

'We're being posted to Baghdad!' I still did not understand. I had not really taken it in that by marrying into the Foreign Service I could so suddenly be whisked away to another part of the world. But it was true – we were off to Baghdad. Stifling a sinking feeling of dread and unaccountable fear, I accepted the fact.

It was our last Sunday in Vienna. We drove into the Wiener Wald. We watched the Russians in their Sunday best walking out with their families. Sailors were all over the place, their ribbons flapping at the back of their caps. As we passed a group, they waved and I waved back.

We had received letters from the former Heads of the Internal Affairs Division, from Brigadier Block, now commanding the Surrey Territorials and from Brigadier Verney, now a Major-General, commanding the London Territorials. Both wrote that they missed 'the mad Russkis', as we called the Russians. We would also miss them – very much. But, I thought to myself, the job I had come out to do was in any case over. The Russians were leaving Austria. We had had our chance – a chance to get to know them, to understand them and their ways, to influence them, to show them our way of life. Now the Iron Curtain would separate us, East and West. Had we failed completely? Had we not managed to pierce numerous holes in it already?

White Among the Reds

By chance we met Captain Beloussov, General Kurasov's ADC. As he said good-bye he asked me: 'Why don't you write about us? You have met us, you have had a chance to understand us. Why don't you write it down, tell others what we are really like?'

It was too late. I told him that having married into the Foreign Service, I was no longer free to write.

On the sleeper carrying us away from Vienna the journey seemed endless as we passed from zone to zone, stopping at each frontier. It was our first journey by train in Austria. We had been warned that people were often hauled off the trains by the Russians, that luggage was looted, passengers insulted and even manhandled by them. It was, we were told, a dangerous way to travel.

At two in the morning we jolted to a halt at the last frontier; we were leaving the Russian zone. Russian military were standing all along the platform. Officers began boarding the train. I removed my wrist watch and hid it under my pillow.

A knock. Alan switched on the light. A smart, slim young Russian officer beamed at us from the doorway. He stretched out his hand. From the lower bunk Alan handed over our papers. Hardly glancing at them, he handed them back. His mouth was twitching as he controlled his amusement at our sleepy, startled faces. He wished us a happy journey, gave a smart salute and was gone.

With shame I drew out my watch; Alan was doing the same. We laughed and settled down again. I dozed. 'We're going away, we're going away . . . away . . . away . . .' the train beat out the words. I was filled with sadness . . . it was all over, finished . . . no more Russkis. . .

But I was no longer alone. I had Alan. Warmth and reassurance flooded over me. I felt a thrill of expectation. Would Baghdad prove exciting? I snuggled down more comfortably. Alan's regular breathing merged with the rhythm of the train, with my own heart beats. I smiled, sighed with contentment and slept.

Senior members of the Allied Commission for Austria referred to in the book

BRITISH ELEMENT
Commander-in-Chief: Lieut-General Sir Richard McCreery succeeded by Lieut-General Sir James Stuart Steele.
Deputy Commander-in-Chief: Maj-General Winterton.
Chief of Staff: Maj-General Packard.
Commandant: Brigadier Palmer succeeded by Brigadier Verney.

SOVIET ELEMENT
Commander-in-Chief: Marshal Koniev succeeded by Col-General Kurasov.
Deputy Commander-in-Chief: Col-General Zheltov.
Chief of Staff: Lieut-General Morozov.
Commandant: Lieut-General Blagodatov succeeded by Lieut-General Lebedenko.

AMERICAN ELEMENT
Commander-in-Chief: General Mark Clark.
Deputy Commander-in-Chief: Maj-General Gruenther.
Commandant: Brigadier-General Lewis.

FRENCH ELEMENT
Commander-in-Chief: General Bethouart.
Deputy Commander-in-Chief: General de Brigade Cherrière.
Commandant: General de Brigade Du Peyrat.

Index

Allied Commission for Austria (ACA), 2, 23, 26, 30, 31, 43, 45, 46, 49, 52–63, 76, 81, 100, 131, 134, 147, 156, 159, 205–6
Bethouart, General, French C-in-C, 45, 70, 185
Bevin, Ernest, British Foreign Secretary, 157, 159–60
Blagodatov, Lieut-Gen., 1st Russian Commandant, 19–20, 26–8, 41, 106, 108
Cherrière, Gen. de Brig., French Deputy C-in-C, 16, 25, 28, 199
Churchill, Winston, 160
Clark, General Mark, American C-in-C, 44–5, 64, 70, 76, 147, 152–3, 167, 170, 180, 187, 195
Du Peyrat, Gen. de Brig., French Commandant, 41, 111, 116–8
Figl, Herr, Chancellor of the Austrian Republic, 70, 170, 208
Gruber, Herr, Foreign Minister of the Austrian Republic, 170, 190
Gruenther, Maj-Gen., American Deputy C-in-C, 16, 52
Harding, Lieut-Gen. Sir John, 182–4
KGB *see* NKVD
Koniev, Marshal, 1st Russian C-in-C, 14, 31, 33, 43, 45, 47, 63–4, 67, 70, 72–4, 76–7, 127, 147–9, 151, 153, 169–70, 172–5, 184, 195, 205
Kurasov, Col-Gen., 2nd Russian C-in-C, 151, 153–4, 173, 175–6, 180–4, 187, 193, 200–1, 206–8, 213
Lebedenko, Lieut-Gen., 2nd Russian Commandant, 106, 108, 110–2, 115–20, 152, 170
Lenin, 18, 28, 73, 99, 173
Lewis, Brig-Gen., American Commandant, 26, 28, 116–7, 119–20
McCreery, Lieut-Gen. Sir Richard, 1st British C-in-C, 14, 31, 43–5, 47, 64, 67–8, 70, 72, 76, 149, 153, 168, 172–4, 177, 184
Morozov, Lieut-Gen., Russian Chief of Staff, 24, 26–9, 41, 64–5, 68–9, 88, 90, 100–2, 119, 163, 205, 208
NKVD (*now* KGB), 22, 65, 89–92, 140, 157
Packard, Maj-Gen., British Chief of Staff, 24, 47, 178–9
Palmer, Brig., 1st British Commandant, 26, 41–2; 106–8, 110
Peniakoff, Lieut-Col. Vladimir, 'Popski' of 'Popski's Private Army', 31, 129, 164, 178
Popski *see* Peniakoff
Renner, Dr Karl, President of the Austrian Republic, 41, 72–3, 142
Stalin, 18, 25, 28, 73, 89, 99, 108, 126, 127, 156, 161, 173
Steele, Lieut-Gen. Sir James Stuart, 2nd British C-in-C, 175–7, 180–5, 187–8, 193, 196, 200, 206–8
Trotsky, 73
Verney, Brig., 2nd British Commandant, 23–4, 53–4, 107, 110, 112–3, 115–20, 177, 213
Vlassov, Russian general captured by Germans and appointed leader of so-called 'Russian Liberation Army', 9, 114–5
Vyshinsky, Russian Deputy Foreign Minister, 159–60
Winterton, Maj-Gen., British Deputy C-in-C, 2, 16–7, 21, 26, 28, 37, 48, 61, 100, 148–54, 157, 161–2, 168–70, 172–5, 187–8, 194, 199, 206, 208
Zheltov, Col-Gen., Russian Deputy C-in-C, 61, 64, 100, 149–50, 152–3, 161, 166, 173–5, 187, 205

216